MURDER
ME
GENTLY

BY

THOMAS ALEXANDER

Murder Me Gently by Thomas Alexander
Direct Light Publications
45 Dudley Court, Endell Street, London, WC2H 9RF

Permissions may be sought directly from Publishing Rights Department 45 Dudley Court, Endell Street, London, WC2H 9RF
performance@directlight-publications.com

Library of Congress Cataloguing in Publication Data
Application submitted.
British Library Cataloguing in Publication Data
Application submitted.
03 04 05 06 07 08 10 9 8 7 6 5 4 3
ISBN 978-1-941979-09-9

–

Edited by Shirin Laghai for Direct Light Publications.

Cover Design by SimplyA

Cover Photograph by Chris Boland
Model: Matt Ray Brown
www.distantcloud.co.uk

Murder Me Gently

SYNOPSIS

Set around the startling true story of the assassination of Russian journalists Alexander Litvinenko and Anna Politkovskaya, Murder Me Gently blends real life events with Film Noir style storytelling to help highlight the human rights abuses and government oppression systemic in modern day Russia.

When a Russian journalist is shot dead on her doorstep, a conman and a spy join forces to wreak revenge on those they consider responsible.

But while all is fair in love and war, little is ever civil in the world of international espionage.

Who is fooling who? Who is on whose side? And what wouldn't you give to torture an ex?

In the classic tradition of Film Noir comes a thriller/comedy that pits lover against lover, friend against foe, and nation against nation in a global game of cat and mouse that will affect us all.

ABOUT THE AUTHOR

Thomas Alexander has worked in almost all forms of theatre, from opera to children's performances, working as everything from stage hand to costume designer, and has seen his work translated into four different languages and performed as far afield as America and Afghanistan.

His plays, along with his first novel, *A Scattering Of Orphans*, have been published by Direct Light Publications.

Also by the Author

PLAYS

Happiness
Murder Me Gently
The Family
Begat
The Crossroads Country
Great
The Visitor
When Dusk Brings Glory
The Recruitment Officer
Writer's Block
The Last Christmas
Writing William
The Big Match

ONE ACT PLAYS

Four Widows and A Funeral
For Arts Sake
The TV
Life TM
The Dance
The Pink Cow

ADAPTATIONS

William Shakespeare's R3
Othello

NOVELS

A Scattering Of Orphans

FOREWORD

You are not allowed to take photos of the grave of Alexander Litvinenko. Under orders from his wife, the tour guides in the cemetery north of London where he has been laid to rest, standing near the graves of such luminaries as Karl Marx and Douglas Adams, ask visitors not to take snaps, but they pause, nonetheless and ask tourists from the USA, Europe, et al, if they know who the man is before regaling them with the story of one of the strangest assassinations of the last century.

But no one tells the story of Anna Politkovskaya, Vyacheslav Yaroshenko, Magomed Yevloyev, Telman Alishayav, and the many other journalists and lawyers assassinated for speaking out about the practices of the Russian government.

I began writing Murder Me Gently during the rehearsal period for the Tokyo production of The Crossroads Country in 2009 following the assassination of human rights lawyers Stanislv Markelov and Annastasia Baburova on a Moscow street. I'd known for some time that I wanted to write about state sovereignty and corporate interests under the guise of some sort of comedy, and as sad as this was it seemed like the perfect opportunity. Like many others, I had been following the progression of Russia under Vladimir Putin into a totalitarian oligarchy with interest, and the assassinations, together with the invasion of Georgia by Russian troops in 2008, convinced me that there was something intrinsically incredulous that needed to be told.

The more I researched, the more I found the world of modern Russian international relations bizarre. From Litzinenko and the strange case of MV Artic Sea – current during the first draft and seemingly boarded and pirated by members of Mossad to prevent its real cargo from reaching Syria – to Vladimir Putin's election to Prime Minister and the installation of the puppet (and, importantly, hirsute) Dmitry Medvedev as President. All of these events seemed more out of the pen of John Le Carre or Graham Green, or even – increasingly – Raymond Chandler than Pravda or The New York Times.

The more outlandish the plots, it appeared, the more likely that they could be true. When Litvinenko and his followers claimed that he had been poisoned by the Russian government with close ties to the mafia the West let out a stifled guffaw, but within months it became clear that this was indeed the case. The invasion of Georgia and the subsequent withdrawal seemed at first to be a case of the right hand not knowing what the left was doing, but quickly became understood as a strategic masterstroke (and one which would be repeated in the Ukraine in 2014).

Russia's approach to world politics and media criticism seemed a plot so ridiculous in nature that it could have been filmed by Howard Hawks, who infamously stated when asked about the plot of The Big Sleep: "Don't ask me, I'm just the director!"

I love Film Noir. It's incredibly fun to write, and I have always been drawn to the kind of failed anti-heroes and destructive personas that populate the genre. It's also not something you often see on stage. Coming into production in Tokyo in 2009 we were broke, and

I knew that I needed something that would work well on a black box stage with minimal props and costumes. That, together with the outlandish acts of the FSB and their close ties with Putin, convinced me that this was the best way to illuminate Russia's human rights abuses and international conflicts, a belief which only increased by the time the play was eventually put on.

Murder Me Gently finally saw production in Cambridge 2011, with a limited run ending in London in 2012. During that time the arrest of Pussy Riot, the assassination of Natalia Estemirova, and beating of Sapiyat Magomedova, amongst many other events, had all caught the world's attention.

Since then, Russia has continued to act globally without impunity, invading the Ukraine in 2013, funding Syria, and banning homosexuals from the Sochi winter Olympics of 2014 where "enforcers" were sent out around the Olympic Village with horsewhips to beat protestors.

I'd like to make a joke about Howard Hawks, but I can't. I'd like to say the West is better, but Edward Snowdon is currently living as an asylum seeker in Moscow. The plot has become too preposterous.

Thomas Alexander – 2014

Cast of Characters

No of cast: 6

HARRY LIME - Conman. No nationality. Thirties.
VIVIAN RUTLEDGE - Interpol Agent. French. Thirties.
ANNA KORENKA - Russian. Female. Does not exist.
VICTOR LAZLO - Russian oligarch. Late 40s upwards.
AGENT QUINLAN - CIA/NSA. Mid thirties.
MR. HAND - Russian Mobster. Physically Imposing.

NOTE: *All characters with the exception of Anna Korenka are named after characters from Film Noir movies. Anna Korenka is named in honour of the real life Russian journalist Anna Politkovskaya.*

MURDER ME GENTLY

Murder Me Gently was originally performed in Cambridge in 2010.

Produced by Crossroads Theatre Company, it was directed by Alec Harris.

ORIGINAL CAST

Harry Lime	Matt Ray Brown
Vivian Rutledge	Helene Salvini-Fujita
Anna Korenka	Genevieve Cleghorn
Victor Lazlo	Alec Harris
Agent Quinlan	Declan Lynch
Mr. Hand	Alan Hays

MURDER ME GENTLY

ACT 1

ACT 1

SCENE 1

FADE IN ON STAGE FRONT, DOWNSTAGE, A SINGLE LIGHT ILLUMINATING A SMALL WRITING DESK.

IT'S RAINING. IT'S ALWAYS RAINING.

ENTER ANNA.

ANNA STEPS INTO THE LIGHT, CALM, SERIOUS.

SHE PICKS UP A DICTAPHONE FROM THE TABLE AND CLICKS IT ON.

ANNA Letter to The Times – London, New York – copies to Economist, La Monde, Pravda. March 9th 2010.

SHE PAUSES, THINKING.

ANNA Details of all proofs are available on the attached server. Records kept at the Gestalt Academy, the Library of Congress, and the British Library can be accessed for verification. My name is Anna Korenka. Until recently I was a journalist working for Vanity Fair magazine on a story about the ties between the CIA and organized crime in the Russian ministry.

PAUSE.

Three months ago today I was shot in the head outside my apartment by someone who, I believe, was working in connection with the Russian mafia, under the guidance of the CIA.

Details of my death, including proof of those responsible are available to anyone upon request. All I require in return... All I ask from my sacrifice... is that the whole truth is printed – without omissions – so that the guilty can be brought to justice and my death and the deaths of so many others like me, will not have been in vain.

PAUSE.

OFF IN THE DARK A CAT MEOWS.

That, and I will need someone to look after the cat.

SCENE 2

LIGHTS UP ON A RESTAURANT. THREE EMPTY TABLES SIT CENTRE STAGE.

HARRY SITS STAGE LEFT HIS BACK TO THE OTHER TABLES. HE IS CONFIDENT. WAITING. QUINLAN APPROACHES HIM DRESSED AS A WAITER.

QUINLAN (RUSSIAN ACCENT) Water?

HARRY Sorry.

QUINLAN Water!

HARRY I think I'm fine.

QUINLAN I clear this away?

HARRY Really, I'm fine.

QUINLAN Okay.

QUINLAN MOVES BACK TO HIS POSITION. VIVIAN ENTERS. QUINLAN, UNSEEN TO HARRY, NODS TOWARDS HIM.

SHE MOVES TOWARDS HARRY, WHO BRIGHTENS, BUT THEN MOVES RIGHT PAST HIM AND SITS AT THE OTHER TABLE.

HARRY PAUSES, THEN TURNS IN HIS CHAIR TO SPEAK TO

HER.

VIVIAN LOOKS AWAY.

HARRY Hi. Um. I think you're at the wrong table.

VIVIAN Pardon?

HARRY I'm pretty sure you're supposed to be sitting next to me.

VIVIAN Désolée, mais je ne parle pas l'anglais.

HARRY (GETTING UP AND GOING TO HER TABLE) Okay, I'm at the wrong table , you don't mind if I join you, do you?

VIVIAN (OVERLAP) Je… Mais que faites-vous? Ne vous asseillez pas. Garçon?

HARRY Interesting. That's not what I'd have gone with

VIVIAN (OVERLAP) Garçon… Ecoutez, je suis désolée, sans doute me prenez-vous pour quelqu'un d'autre, je n'en sais rien, enfin, cela m'est égal, en tout cas, écoutez-moi! je ne suis vraiment pas intéressée. Okay?

HARRY I'm sorry, I don't speak French. That is French, isn't it?

VIVIAN Oh mon Dieu. Allez-vous-en, petit homme stupide.

HARRY Greek, yes. Spanish at a push. Lithuanian, Dutch, Arabic. French? No. Could you pass me the water?

VIVIAN Vous comptez vraiment rester ici? Garçon. Je ne suis pas intéressée par vous, vous comprenez? Peut-être que vous attirez d'autres personnes, j'en sais rien. Peut-être que vous êtes intéressant ou charmant, comment le saurais-je. Vous n'avez pas l'air méchant, mais s'il vous plaît, je vous en supplie, allez-vous-en. Garçon!

HARRY (BEAT) Yeah, I'm going to just assume you asked me to share a meal with you. Waiter?

AT HARRY'S CALL QUINLAN COMES OVER.

VIVIAN Il s'est permis de s'asseoir ici. Je ne le connais pas et je n'ai pas envie de lui ici. S'il vous plaît, dites-lui de partir.

HARRY Hi. A bottle of Chateau Rothschild 1987, '85 if you have it.

QUINLAN Um…

VIVIAN Mais ne restez pas planté comme ça! Faites-le partir. Je ne le veux pas ici. Vous comprenez?

HARRY It's our anniversary, she gets a little emotional. Anything but eighty eight would be fine.

QUINLAN Sir.

QUINLAN WITHDRAWS.

HARRY Seems he doesn't speak French either. (TAKING A BREAD ROLL) Are you eating these? I'm famished. You don't mind do you?

VIVIAN Merde! Mais allez-vous-en! Vous ne comprenez pas, je ne vous veux pas ici. Je ne vous connais pas et je ne veux pas vous connaître. Regardez-vous, vous êtes ridicule! Vous croyez avoir l'air beau comme ca? Vous l'avez pris des étagères, n'est-ce-pas? C'est quoi ce look d'intellectuel milliardaire, de 'je suis trop cool pour me soucier de quoi j'ai l'air'? C'est ça non? Vous êtes ridicule. Dites-moi, ca marche vraiment sur les femmes tout ça?

HARRY You are so turning me on right now. Alright. You want to play it this way, fine, this is how you want to play it. I'll play along.

VIVIAN Je doute que vous ne sachiez comment satisfaire une femme.

HARRY You don't speak English.

VIVIAN Tout est la même chose pour vous. D'ailleurs, vous êtes quoi, américain, non? Ne me dites pas anglais, oh mon Dieu, un anglais. Pire que les américains, il n'y a que les anglais.

HARRY And we haven't met. Is that the rules of the game?

VIVIAN Mais peut-être que vous avez tous un petit pénis, j'en sais rien. C'est pour ça que vous pleurez votre maman la nuit. Ah oui, jadis vous étiez une grande nation, mais maintenant? La Grande-Bretagne? Plutôt la 'Petite Bretagne'.

HARRY So… You won't understand me if I tell you how incredible you look tonight. How outstandingly hot you look in that dress, with the neck and the décolletage.

VIVIAN (COVERING HERSELF) Je parie qu'elles vous quittent toujours, non? Après qu'elles aient vu… enfin, quoiqu'il en soit, elles s'en vont, et vous laissent vous, dans votre grand lit, avec votre petit pénis.

HARRY No? Okay. And you don't remember… Istanbul? Was that a smile? Against the wall of the Blue Mosque? Nothing.

VIVIAN Ecoutez-vous, comme vous fuyez. Mais quelle laideur cette langue! On dirait que vous mâchez du chewing gum.

HARRY (PAUSE) I could take you outside. Now. I could take you outside and by the time we're finished, I'd be fluent in French, that's how incredible you look to me, that's how much you turn me on right now. I could take you outside, throw you against the bonnet of my Lamborghini and press my mouth to your exposed breast and I bet you, pounds to euro, that by the time I pull your hair back and push my fingers into your mouth. I'd be almost fluent.

VIVIAN (SWITCHING TO ENGLISH) You do not have a Lamborghini.

HARRY Want me to get one?

VIVIAN So crude.

HARRY You love me for it.

QUINLAN ENTERS WITH THE BOTTLE AND TWO GLASSES. THE TWO STARE AT EACH OTHER AS HE PLACES THE GLASSES ON THE TABLE.

QUINLAN 1988, sir.

HARRY (TAKING THE BOTTLE) No, that's fine, I'll open it.

HE MOTIONS FOR THE CORKSCREW. QUINLAN LOOKS AT VIVIAN WHO DOESN'T REACT, AND THEN HANDS IT TO HIM, KNOCKING OVER A GLASS, CAREFULLY PLACED BY HARRY.

HARRY Oh dear.

QUINLAN I… I am very sorry, I'll get you another one.

VIVIAN Please, leave it, it is nothing.

QUINLAN No, no. Sir, madam. It is totally my fault, I will get you another.

HARRY LEANS ACROSS AND STEALS VIVIAN'S.

HARRY Take your time. We'll start with this, shall we?

QUINLAN Er… I'll bring you another.

VIVIAN Just go.

HARRY POURS A GLASS FOR HIMSELF.

HARRY So you do speak English.

VIVIAN Of course I speak English. Monkeys can speak English. It is the language of monkeys and crude people.

HARRY So, just to play along for a minute…

VIVIAN I wanted you to go away.

HARRY Wanted?

VIVIAN Want.

HARRY You said wanted!

VIVIAN In any tense, you not being here is the preferable outcome.

HARRY And what would be?

VIVIAN You. Gone. Preferably dead in an alley somewhere.

HARRY I walked right into that one.

VIVIAN And now you can walk out of this. Goodbye.

HARRY Why did you pretend you didn't know me?

VIVIAN I am not here for you.

HARRY You're not here for me?

VIVIAN There in an echo coming off your empty skull. (BEAT) Go away. I am bored with you.

HARRY I think you missed me.

VIVIAN I most certainly did not.

HARRY I think you couldn't stay away. All that space out there without me in it.

VIVIAN You really are the most annoying man, you know that?

HARRY To my credit. I do. I think you missed me, couldn't stand to be without me, and now you've come to say you're sorry.

VIVIAN Sorry?

HARRY You're forgiven.

VIVIAN I mean sorry 'what', not sorry… I am on a job.

HARRY Oh, I know you're on a job.

VIVIAN You are, most certainly, not the job.

QUINLAN Madam.

HARRY I'm glad to hear it. Here's your glass.

HARRY TAKES THE GLASS FROM HER AND POURS SOME WINE, HANDING IT OVER THE TABLE. SHE LOOKS AT HIM FOR A SECOND, THEN THROW THE WINE IN HIS FACE, TAKES THE BOTTLE AND POURS FOR HERSELF.

HARRY Yeah, you'd better pour.

QUINLAN Erm. Perhaps you'd like to order.

VIVIAN We won't be eating.

QUINLAN Madam?

HARRY She never eats in foreign restaurants, don't trust them. Food might be poisoned.

QUINLAN I can assure you…

VIVIAN Leave us.

EXIT QUINLAN.

HARRY I like him.

VIVIAN What have I got to be sorry for?

HARRY Well, Istanbul for starters.

VIVIAN Yes, you mentioned Istanbul before.

HARRY You mean before when I was dry and you were pretending we didn't know each other.

VIVIAN What are you saying; something happened between us, in Istanbul?

HARRY I think we've done the forgetting thing already.

VIVIAN I've been to Istanbul hundreds of times.

HARRY (BEAT) That's pretty cold. Even for you, that's pretty cold.

VIVIAN I… What is your name?

HARRY Like you've forgotten.

VIVIAN Like I'd remember.

HARRY (PAUSE) Lime. Harry Lime.

VIVIAN (BEAT) Yes, well, I'm sorry. 'Harry'. But, no. We shared something? How nice for you. I share lots of things. I'm a giving person.

HARRY Okay, that's the way you want to play it.

VIVIAN (LAUGHING) Okay.

HARRY So, what? You don't remember me, is that it? No, you remember me, but don't remember. You've forgotten me but you haven't forgotten.

VIVIAN Pretty much forgotten, I'm afraid.

HARRY That's pretty cold, even for you.

VIVIAN I guess I must be a cold person then.

HARRY Feet, yes. Hands, certainly, but heart. Never.

VIVIAN I had an upgrade.

HARRY Yes, I really don't see what the upside is here. You clearly remember who I am…

VIVIAN (BEAT) Look at you? Is that all it takes? Is your ego bruised? What a little boy. Would you prefer I pretended I remember you? Oh, you were magnificent. A stallion! I dreamed about you for weeks.

HARRY You're lying.

VIVIAN Of course I'm lying, I can't even remember who you are. (HARRY GETS UP) Oh, you're going? Au revoir. Please, give my regards to all the other women who have forgotten what you are like in bed.

HARRY God, you're a magnificent bitch.

VIVIAN Woof.

HARRY I am going to go to the toilet, and when I come back… The salt cellar is three centimetres from the pepper, the pepper is four centimetres from the flowers. There are three flowers. The table cloth is white, your eyes are hazel and, what I'm saying is, when I come back; all those things better be the same.

VIVIAN I told you. You're not the job!

HARRY Good. Then I can pee in safety, can't I? And whatever little game you're playing. Why-ever you're here… It's good to see you Vivian. Really, really good.

EXIT HARRY.

SCENE 3

TWO WEEKS BEFORE. VIVIAN AS BEFORE.

QUINLAN ENTERS, DRESSED IN A SUIT.

QUINLAN (INTO HIS ARMBAND) Target is clear. I'm going in.

VIVIAN Excuse me.

QUINLAN   Ms. Rutledge? You mind if I sit?

VIVIAN What is this?

QUINLAN (LOOKING AT HER FOOD) God, that looks good. I haven't eaten in, like hours, you mind.

VIVIAN (RISING TO LEAVE) You think…

QUINLAN (GRABBING HER WRIST AND PRODUCING A BADGE) Sit, seriously, sit.

VIVIAN Homeland Security?

QUINLAN You know what, this isn't bad!

VIVIAN So, you're the people following me.

QUINLAN   No, that would be the FBI.

VIVIAN And the heavy breathing on the phone?

QUINLAN   That's the CIA.

VIVIAN Then what are you?

QUINLAN   We're the good guys, Vivian. You don't mind if I call you Vivian, do you?

VIVIAN Not at all. You don't mind if I call you an ass?

QUINLAN   I've been called worse.

VIVIAN You do realize you are blowing two months of covert ops? I am this close to…

QUINLAN   You're this close to getting your head blown off is what you're getting. Johnny Reno? The guy you're meeting? We picked him up an hour ago. Possession. Not sexy. Not, you know, smuggling weapons of mass media into the country or anything, but he's going away anyway so what the hell. Of course, when his 'cohorts' start to wonder why he's not around anymore they're going to check everything. Probably doing it already, and when they realize that not only are you not a Vegas showgirl from Ontario but an Interpol agent operating, may I say, outside the purview of United States law, they're going to a) kill you, or b) kill you. I am of course exaggerating. Fine piece like you they're not going to kill until they've turned you into the best ride in Vegas. This pasta sauce is out of this world!

VIVIAN You're a real people person, aren't you?

QUINLAN   I do what I can. (PRODUCING A PHOTO FROM A POCKET) You know who this is?

VIVIAN Listen, Agent...

QUINLAN   Quinlan, ma'am

VIVIAN   Don't ma'am me, Agent Quinlan.

QUINLAN Yes, ma'am. You know who this is?

VIVIAN Never seen him before in my life.

QUINLAN Hmm. You're good. And I'm not the kind of person who thinks good exists, but you're good. You looked right at that photo and you didn't blink. Most people look away, you know that? They see a photo of a person they know and asked to identify it they look away. You, not so much as a flicker. You, Agent Vivian Rutledge of Interpol, are one hell of a piece of work. I can see why the director held out a full hour before giving you up. Still, you are French. Giving up was kind of a foregone conclusion.

VIVIAN I don't have to be here.

QUINLAN Yeah, you do! See, you are a) in the country illegally under a false passport, and b) were about to arrest and, well, let's call it kidnap, shall we? You were about to kidnap an American national, a scumbag American national but an American national nonetheless, and ship him overseas on a, what was it? A fishing trawler?

VIVIAN He is wanted for crimes against France.

QUINLAN Yeah, but that's not, like, a real crime is it. Who hasn't wanted to commit crimes against France at one time or another? So, the picture. Who is he?

VIVIAN I honestly don't know.

QUINLAN (REVEALING HIS GUN ONCE MORE) Please. Don't make me fill out the paperwork!

VIVIAN We've met eight times. Paris, Switzerland, Denmark, but you know all this.

QUINLAN Tell me anyway.

VIVIAN Last time was Istanbul. He was using the name Freud.

QUINLAN Original.

VIVIAN Time before that it was Bergerac. He's a got a thing for historical characters.

QUINLAN Bergerac?

VIVIAN Cyrano.

QUINLAN Go on.

VIVIAN That's all I know. He's a thief, a confidence trickster.

QUINLAN Which one, a thief or a confidence trickster?

VIVIAN What's the difference? He plays the long con. Big stakes. The kind they don't play anymore. You remember that thing with the space shuttle?

QUINLAN The bidding war on Atlantis?

VIVIAN That was him. Set up a meet in Istanbul. Sold it for two hundred million with launch rights to the North Koreans. What do the American government want with him?

QUINLAN This was taken four days ago. In France. This is a safe deposit box in the Marseilles branch of Banc Frances. It appears he rented a safety deposit box, then used the time he had with it to pick the lock on the safety deposit box next to it. Which, by the way, are supposed to be unpickable.

VIVIAN He's an expert at locks.

QUINLAN That's not in the file!

VIVIAN His uncle Felix. He was a master cat burglar. Taught him everything he knew.

QUINLAN Is that so?

VIVIAN Raised him as a child.

QUINLAN What else wasn't in his file?

VIVIAN He has a mole on his left buttock. It looks like the queen.

QUINLAN You always 'get intimate' to the people you're trying to arrest?

VIVIAN (SHRUGS) They are slightly more interesting that the people trying to arrest me.

QUINLAN That so? Anyway, like I said, he used the time at the bank to break into another safety deposit box and steal the contents.

VIVIAN Bonds? Nazi jewellery?

QUINLAN Baridium.

VIVIAN Baridium?

QUINLAN Baridium.

VIVIAN What's that?

QUINLAN I look like a metallurgist to you? It's some kind of rare compound. It was kept there by a company called Inventec.

VIVIAN Really? And what has any of this got to do with me?

QUINLAN You're going to help bring him in!

SCENE 4

ENTER ANNA, A TIN OF CAT FOOD IN HER HAND.

ANNA   Here, kitty, kitty.

ANNA   Fuck it.

SHE PULLS OUT A PHONE.

ANNA (INTO PHONE) No, I'm here now. Yeah. I think the cat's dead. (PAUSE) I tried that. (PAUSE) I'm not going to try that! (PAUSE) Because I'm not a twelve year old girl, that's why. (BEAT) No. (BEAT) Because I say so! (BEAT) Fine. (TO THE ROOM) Kitten want yum yums! (INTO PHONE) Happy? (BEAT) You've got to be kidding me. (TO THE ROOM) Kitten want fishy yum yums! This is besides the point, do you have something for me or not? (WRITING) Yeah, Okay, that's good. How do you spell that? (PAUSE) As in Hugo? Alright. (PAUSE) I've heard of him. When will you get here? Shit. No, I have to be in Scotland. Short play. You can't get here earlier? No, I understand. Reuters, yeah. Yes. Yes. I will. Yes, I promise! I will!!! I'll look for the damn cat before I go, alright? Fine. Yes. Uh huh. I'll look for the cat before I go, promise. Yes, you too.

SHE PUTS THE PHONE AWAY AND PULLS OUT A VOICE RECORDER.

ANNA (CONT.) Anna files 287. Continued. Transpose and edit. (PAUSE) Continued from previous paragraph… The question is not however, whether South Ossetia wants independence, or even whether Putin's oil deals are in the best interests of the Russian people. It's the methods that are used and the government culpability in those methods that raises eyebrows in the West. An increasing alliance with former cold war criminals and post-communist mafia bosses show… no, strike that… suggest either a familiarity with, or a frightening lack of distrust in black market racketeers and blood stained oil barons. More frightening still however, is the West's ambivalent attitude to such alliances, with either a blind eye or a blank check given to anyone with even the most fragile stamp of government approval. (PAUSE) Victor Lazlo…

BLACKOUT.

THUNDER BREAKS.

THE SOUND OF RAIN FADES.

SCENE 5

VIVIAN IS ON THE PHONE. QUINLAN CROSSES AND GLARES AT HER.

HARRY RETAKES HIS PLACE AT THE TABLE. SHE MOTIONS FOR HIM TO WAIT.

VIVIAN (INTO PHONE) Non. (AND CLICKS IT OFF AGAIN) Where were we?

HARRY Istanbul, throwing wine in my face. Not here for me.

VIVIAN I had to make a call.

HARRY Mother? Give her my love.

VIVIAN What do you know about my mother?

HARRY I know she's a fifty year old C-rated fashion designer who collects twenty year old boys in the way other women collect cats. I read your file.

VIVIAN You did not read my file.

HARRY Three citations for violence? Really? You?

VIVIAN How did you get my file?

HARRY It's Interpol. I hired a twelve year old kid to hack into your database.

VIVIAN You do realize I could kill you right now and just make up a reason.

HARRY Why do you think I'm not drinking the wine. (OFF) Waiter!

ENTER QUINLAN.

HARRY (CONT.) Are you seeing anyone? (TO QUINLAN) This was the eighty eight. I specifically asked for anything but the eighty eight. Let's try that again, shall we? Eighty sevens have a much better throwing arm. (TO VIVIAN) You didn't answer the question.

VIVIAN It's none of your business.

HARRY (TO QUINLAN) Make that eighty six. (TO VIVIAN) Someone I know then. Ireland? Jones. Not Davis... Davis! You're seeing Davis? Really? You're dating your boss?

EXIT QUINLAN.

VIVIAN He's twice the man you are.

HARRY I always thought he was gay.

VIVIAN He is not gay!

HARRY Are you sure? He's very effeminate.

VIVIAN He happens to be very physical!

HARRY He'd have to be! Does he still check himself in every reflective surface?

VIVIAN He takes pride his appearance.

HARRY Gay.

VIVIAN You are such a child!

HARRY You know, it's okay to admit you missed me.

VIVIAN You really haven't changed, have you? You're still a puerile little boy playing at the real world.

HARRY And you're still a bitch with daddy issues; it all works out.

VIVIAN How do you live with yourself?

HARRY How do you live without me?

PAUSE.

VIVIAN Happily, as in, ever after.

HARRY Had to think about it though. So, what are you here for?

ENTER LAZLO AND HAND.

VIVIAN Same reason you are.

LAZLO AND HAND SIT AT THE OTHER TABLE.

LAZLO Waiter!

HARRY (TO VIVIAN) You need to leave.

LAZLO (TO QUINLAN) Borscht.

VIVIAN And why's that?

QUINLAN This is a French restaurant, sir.

LAZLO And this is Russia. For me, you make borscht. Vodka. Not for him, he doesn't drink.

HARRY There are not people you want to be dealing with!

VIVIAN Then why are you here? You have, maybe, business?

HARRY You really ready for these waters, little fish?

LAZLO Mr. Hand. I do not understand French food. It is indulgence. Rich. Oils. It is for people who have too much time, too many desires, this is what I think. A man must control two things. His desires, and his time. These things are very valuable to me, you understand? Time?

QUINLAN ENTERS.

VIVIAN (GETTING UP) I'll give you one chance. Come in now. Give us the baridium and I'll go easy on you.

SCENE 6

QUINLAN About time.

VIVIAN Traffic.

QUINLAN I thought maybe you'd decided to stay in L.A. Take up mime.

VIVIAN Where's your source?

QUINLAN Toilet.

VIVIAN Isn't that what got him into trouble in the first place?

ENTER LAZLO.

LAZLO How do you people live like this? No bidet, single ply toilet paper!

QUINLAN Agent Rutledge, Victor Lazlo.

VIVIAN (TO QUINLAN) Can I have a quick word with you? (TO LAZLO) Excuse me.

QUINLAN (TO LAZLO) One second.

THEY WITHDRAW.

VIVIAN This man is a mass murderer! You know he was responsible for Anna Korenka, Alexander Litvinenko...

QUINLAN Mr. Lazlo is a person of extreme interest to the United States.

VIVIAN (BEAT) I'm not even sure what that means.

QUINLAN It means, yes, he's a scumbag, but he's a rich scumbag with oil connections and the rest of us live in the real world. Get over it. (RETURNING TO LAZLO) Mr. Lazlo is the owner of Gia-Nueovo. Gia-Nueovo is the parent company of LDC Dynamics. LDC Dynamics owns Baker's Dozen, they do those dough balls with the sour cream, very good, and Baker's Dozen owns majority shares in...

VIVIAN Inventec.

QUINLAN Exactly.

VIVIAN Fine. But he's your pigeon, okay?

QUINLAN I am happy to help in any way I can.

VIVIAN Alright, Mr. Lazlo, let me ask you this. Why were you storing a semi-precious metal in a lock box in a Marseilles bank?

LAZLO It is a free world. Well, it is for me at any rate. For you, not so much I think Agent Rutting. (TO QUINLAN) I do not like her tone. It is disrespectful.

QUINLAN Mr. Lazlo was approached two days ago by your friend; he introduced himself as Harry Lime.

LAZLO A fictional name, obviously.

QUINLAN Obviously. Lime offered to sell the rock back to Mr. Lazlo, for what we'll call an exaggerated price.

LAZLO Imagine this. The man who stole it! Selling it back to me!

VIVIAN How much was he asking?

QUINLAN Thirty million dollars.

VIVIAN What's it worth?

LAZLO I bought it on eBay. One hundred and twenty-seven dollars, plus shipping. A good price I think.

VIVIAN Then why..?

LAZLO Do you know anything about commodities, Ms. Rutledge?

VIVIAN Agent.

LAZLO Why is gold expensive?

VIVIAN It's rare.

LAZLO Rare? I do not think so. Every jewellers on every high street in the world has it. This is not rare. A twenty goal a season striker, that is rare. Gold, not so much. Gold is expensive because people think it is expensive. They will pay much for it, because of this. They will pay and so it is expensive. When a man goes to considerable lengths to steal a piece of meteor rock and then tries to sell it back to me for thirty million dollars then it is worth at least ten. Price is demand, Ms. Rutledge. What we want, others will buy and buy to stop us having. This is what they mean by supply and demand.

QUINLAN Mr. Lazlo would like our help in getting the baridium back.

VIVIAN Just pay him the money if you think it's worth it.

LAZLO I am business man, Ms. Rutledge. I do business. I do not do blackmail. If a man sells me a rock he stole from me, tomorrow everyone will try to sell me back socks that went missing in the wash. Now, Agent Quinlan, I have a meeting in Dallas. If you will excuse me.

QUINLAN We have a chopper waiting outside. Thank you for your help Mr. Lazlo. The director wanted me to extend his thanks.

LAZLO Okay.

QUINLAN We'll be in touch.

EXIT LAZLO.

VIVIAN You know what he did to him? Alexander Litvinenko. He poisoned him. Over a period of six months. He poisoned him! Perhaps with this exact piece of meteor rock he was hiding in Marseilles!

QUINLAN Baridium isn't radioactive.

VIVIAN What is it then?

QUINLAN Baridium is an alien compound. And when I say alien, I mean Ridley Scott alien, not James Cameron. It is, in fact, not unlike lead. Except where lead 'digests' radioactivity, baridium ingests all known forms of radio waves.

VIVIAN Where are you getting this?

QUINLAN Hand to god? Wikipedia.

VIVIAN And what has all this got to do with the U.S. government?

QUINLAN How much do you know about Russian journalism?

SCENE 7

ANNA ENTERS. SHE'S ALREADY GOT THE RECORDER ON AND IS DICTATING, BUT WHILE SHE DOES SHE HAPPILY SPREADS SOFT PORN MAGAZINES OVER THE FLOOR, BEING CAREFUL TO SPREAD THEM PROVOCATIVELY, IN OBVIOUS PLACES. SHE ALSO THROWS AROUND A COUPLE OF CONDOMS AND A PAIR OF PANTIES.

THESE ACTIONS BRING HER GREAT ENJOYMENT.

ANNA Unlike countries like America, Germany, and even, occasionally, England, Russia's press are on the whole in the pockets of the government and the government, in bed with big business.

LIGHTS UP ON QUINLAN.

QUINLAN DRESSED AS THE WAITER IS OFF HAVING A CIGARETTE STAGE LEFT.

HARRY LEAVES HIS TABLE AND GOES TO JOIN HIM.

ANNA (CONT.) Pressure on foreign newspapers may come in the form of corporate finances but internally it's more often in the form of arrests by police, beatings, and, increasingly, murder.

HARRY Women.

QUINLAN Eh?

HARRY OFFERS TO LIGHT A NEW CIGARETTE. QUINLAN OBLIGES AND THEN PASSES OUT. HARRY DRAGS HIS BODY UNDER THE THIRD UNOCCUPIED TABLE.

ANNA Vyacheslav Yaroshenko, Magomed Yevloyev, Telman Alishayav, Stanislav Markelov... All reporters who spoke out against human rights abuses by government agencies. All shot or beaten to death. Yevloyev, a prominent critic of the Kremlin, was shot while in police custody. Apparently he tried to grab a gun and accidentally shot himself in the temple. Yaroshenko was found beaten into a coma outside his apartment but police claimed no crime was perpetrated. Apparently he'd beaten his own head in. He was editor of the aptly named Crime and Punishment...

(FINISHED SHE LOOKS AROUND) Personal note. Sorry love. Excuse the mess. No time to tidy up.

EXIT ANNA.

SCENE 8

ENTER VIVIAN, QUINLAN.

VIVIAN Sneaky son of a bitch!

QUINLAN What do you mean?

VIVIAN You're not actually buying any of this are you?

QUINLAN Um… Well…

VIVIAN How long have we been spying on Lazlo?

QUINLAN Well, we is…

VIVIAN What is it, a deal? Some secret deal with a U.S. oil company?

QUINLAN Alright, listen…

VIVIAN Son of a bitch!

QUINLAN Lazlo?

VIVIAN Gatsby… Lime! Whatever his name is.

QUINLAN Slow down.

VIVIAN What the hell is Lazlo doing in America?

QUINLAN That's need to know.

VIVIAN Yeah, well, right now you need me to know! You've been using Echelon to spy on Lazlo, right?

QUINLAN Echelon is an inter-continental resource, France included!

VIVIAN Imbecile. If Lazlo knew what the baridium could do, do you think he would have allowed you to spy on him? Do you? Lime is going to give him the rock back, he's going to tell him what it can do! You want me to get you Lime, you've got to let me inside! Now.

QUINLAN'S PHONE RINGS. HE PULLS IT OUT.

QUINLAN (INTO THE PHONE) Yes, sir. (PAUSE) Sir, I don't... (PAUSE) Yes, sir.

HE SHUTS OFF THE PHONE.

VIVIAN Well?

QUINLAN Two weeks from now, Lazlo is going to announce that he's bought an American oil company called Transfield.

VIVIAN Dallas?

QUINLAN Exactly. Transfield are a small to growing company who, however, have extensive contracts in, among other places…

VIVIAN Georgia.

QUINLAN That's very…

VIVIAN Annoying? Sorry, go on.

QUINLAN We want Lazlo to buy Transfield.

VIVIAN Why on earth would you want that?

QUINLAN That's classified.

VIVIAN So the other buyer is…

QUINLAN The Chinese.

VIVIAN Merde!

QUINLAN Look, we don't like this any more than you! This will make Lazlo's friends some of the most powerful people on the face of the earth but the alternative means the Chinese get the benefit of the Siberian oil fields. We don't want that.

VIVIAN China's too strong.

QUINLAN That and we want them to buy their oil from our new interests in…

VIVIAN Iraq.

QUINLAN Exactly.

VIVIAN So, what? Unocal pick up the phone and ask the director of the CIA to use Echelon to spy on a private citizen so they don't lose out to a rival? That is what you are using the most sophisticated spying technology in the world for now, is it?

QUINLAN Not us. You. Where do you think the intercepts came from?

VIVIAN Marseilles!

QUINLAN Bingo.

VIVIAN It's a double bind! Either Lazlo didn't know what the metal could do, or he couldn't build a machine to use it. Lime on the other hand, obviously does know what the metal's for, so either he's about to tell Lazlo…

QUINLAN (THE PENNY DROPS) Or he already has!

VIVIAN Hence the thirty million.

QUINLAN Yeah, okay, but he doesn't know we know what the metal can do.

VIVIAN (BEAT) I thought you said you got it off the internet.

QUINLAN Okay, so he knows we know what the metal can do, which means…

VIVIAN It's the oldest con in the book! You play poker? You have a losing hand, you can't beat the man you want to beat, so you show your hand to the person who can.

QUINLAN This is making my head spin.

VIVIAN If he gets the baridium back, he knows we can no longer spy on him.

QUINLAN Then we have to make sure he never gets the baridium back.

VIVIAN It doesn't matter.

QUINLAN Why not.

VIVIAN How much baridium does it take to make a trigger?

QUINLAN No one knows.

VIVIAN And how much baridium was in the safety deposit box?

QUINLAN Damn it!

VIVIAN Oui. We have to assume he has more. He just let us know that he has a way to disrupt our entire spy networks and he did it while getting us to do his dirty work for him. Either way, I'd pull your surveillance off him right now.

QUINLAN Wait: you think they're in this together, don't you?

VIVIAN My guess is that there never was any baridium in the safety deposit box. My guess is that they don't know how to make the trigger and my guess is that this whole thing is a one large con they're playing on the U.S. government.

QUINLAN You're kidding me?

VIVIAN That's what Lime does. He plays people. Gives them what they want. Which is usually greed. You can't con an honest man.

QUINLAN You've obviously never been to church.

VIVIAN My bet is Lazlo and Lime are in this together. The only question remaining is, who's pulling the strings.

SCENE 9

ENTER LAZLO AND HAND STAGE RIGHT.

WE HEAR THE SOUND OF A CAR APPROACHING ON GRAVEL. HEADLIGHTS SWEEP THE PAIR AND THE ENGINE DIES.

(OFF) HARRY GETS OUT OF THE CAR.

HARRY (OFF) That you, Victor?

LAZLO You were expecting Sepp Blatter, perhaps?

THERE'S NO ANSWER. THE CAR DOOR SLAMS AND HARRY ENTERS.

BOTH LAZLO AND HARRY ARE CARRYING BRIEFCASES. LAZLO'S IS BIGGER.

HARRY Victor.

LAZLO Mr. Lime. This is my associate. Mr. Hand.

HARRY Hand? What's his first name, finger?

LAZLO Fist. You bring contracts?

HARRY I did. Yes. Though really, the need for us to meet here…

LAZLO This is illegal thing, yes? It is not, as you say, kosher.

HARRY Well… I'm C of E so...

LAZLO It is best done in illegal place.

HARRY It's a river.

LAZLO Yes. You should see bodies floating down it at dawn. I am respectable business man these days, this is what they tell me. My office is for respectable people, respectable things. Everything has place.

HARRY You brought the money?

LAZLO I have what is promised. Yes.

HARRY Thirty five million in cash?

LAZLO And for this I get…?

HARRY Arsenal Football Club. Absolutely.

LAZLO I get Dennis Bergkamp?

HARRY You get..?

LAZLO Ah! Ah! I am joking with you, yes? You think I am ignorant bolshevik, eh, eh?

HARRY Right.

LAZLO Bergkamp plays for Tottenham. (BEAT) Nah, ha! I am fucking with you again! (TO HAND) You see the look on his face? I love this man. (TO HARRY) Give him the contract.

HARRY REACHES INTO HIS BRIEFCASE AND PULLS OUT A CONTRACT, HANDING IT TO HAND WHO READS IT CAREFULLY.

HARRY He checks your contracts for you?

LAZLO Mr. Hand? Mr. Hand is first class lawyer! What school did you graduate from again, Mr. Hand?

HAND Harvard.

LAZLO Ten years he is in America, you believe this? Never they think he is Russian spy. Big thing on wrestling circuit!

HARRY Is that right?

LAZLO Two things are hard to find in this world. Good lawyer. Good bodyguard. You find both in one man, you do not let him go. Well, that and good hooker. Hooker is very hard to find. The skill has gone right out of it. But, lawyer, bone-breaker, this is close second. (PAUSE) Arsenal. This is good team? No, doesn't matter. I am the only one they don't let buy an English club, you know this? Abramovitch? I know him when is little boy, piss his pants. Him, they let in. Me, ETA block.

HARRY FIFA.

LAZLO What I say?

HARRY ETA.

LAZLO What's that?

HAND Spanish terrorist cell.

LAZLO Oh, yes. Man, I am bad with words today. FIFA. FIFA will not let me buy. ETA let me buy no problem. Guns, drugs…

HAND It's all here.

LAZLO (SIGNING) Good, good.

HARRY Excellent. If you… Yes, just there. There as well. Alright. So, just to recap. The agents will hold the contract for two months until the board meeting on the 20th. They will then unanimously vote to sell the club to your private consortium for an additional one hundred million. FIFA can stop you coming in with a bid, but they can't stop the club approaching you.

LAZLO This is very good.

HARRY You brought the funds, I take it?

LAZLO Mr. Hand!

HAND HANDS HIM THE BAG

HARRY You won't mind if I count it.

LAZLO I would expect nothing else.

HARRY OPENS THE BAG AND PULLS OUT GYM CLOTHES.

HARRY Another one of your little jokes perhaps?

LAZLO No. Laundry. My wife's, actually, she will want them back. I wanted to do that fake money thing, with the newspapers, all cut into strips, but it is print holiday and I was on a bit of a deadline, so…

HARRY We had an agreement!

LAZLO You think I am stupid. You think I am… schmill, schmeg... (TO HAND) What is the word?

HAND Schmendrik.

LAZLO You think I am schmedrik?! Arsenal football club! Arsenal! You are very stupid man to come here and try to fool me. Good, yes. Almost you had me, but stupid. And now dead.

HAND REACHES OUT TO HARRY WHO REACHES INTO HIS POCKET.

HARRY Hold it right there! I have a gun, and I'm not afraid to use it!

LAZLO (PAUSE) Really?

HARRY OK, I can't back that up.

HAND PUNCHES HIM IN THE FACE.

HARRY (CONT.) Jesus!

HAND HITS HARRY IN FACE AGAIN.

HARRY Ow! Hey! You know how much dental costs?

HAND SWINGS AGAIN. HARRY SKIPS BACK.

HARRY HITS OUT. HAND CATCHES HIS FIST IN HIS PALM AND TWISTS HIS ARM BEHIND HIS BACK.

LAZLO Very stupid man! You know how I know?

HARRY When Thierry Henry offered to wash your car for you?

LAZLO Funny man. (HAND HURTS HIM) Now, that is funny. For you, not so much, but for me, laugh riot! No, I knew when you said FIFA controls the buying of clubs. You think this isn't something I check? UEFA, not FIFA, you stupid little man.

HAND HURTS HIM.

LAZLO Yes. See. Not so witty now. No?

HARRY If you expect me to beg...

LAZLO No, Mr. Lime. I expect you to die. Hah. You know how long I've waited to say that!!! That is great line. "You expect me to beg." "No, Mr. Bond, I expect you to die!" (TO HAND) That almost makes it worth it, don't you think? No? You have no sense of humour. We talk about this, yes? Humour? It is. Okay, okay, we talk, yes? Where was I? (TO HARRY) No, you do not kill the dog that tries to bite you. You, my friend are a genius and you do not kill genius. Fools you kill. Genius you make into your bitch.

HARRY You want me to work for you?

LAZLO You are artist! Selling Arsenal football to one of the world's richest, most dangerous men, this is artist work! I need an artist of your talents. (TO HAND) Let him go.

HARRY So, what? You want me to steal the Mona Lisa or something?

LAZLO I have wife. What I want another depressing woman for? No, no. I want you to steal one thing money cannot buy.

HARRY Love?

LAZLO Ha. No. Love is easy. Privacy. I want you to steal my privacy back from the C.I.A.!

SCENE 10

VIVIAN (BEAT) I'll need access to all the Echelon records on Lazlo. If he knows we're watching him we need to see where and when he figured it out.

QUINLAN That can be arranged.

VIVIAN And we need to monitor his bank accounts.

QUINLAN Why?

VIVIAN Because if Lime is setting this whole thing up, then Lazlo would have had to pay him. A lot.

QUINLAN Thirty million a lot?

VIVIAN At least.

QUINLAN Good thinking. So Lime is the key.

VIVIAN We need to know what he knows. And quickly. We need to get the baridium secured and we need to do all this while not letting Lazlo know we're on to him. Lime's the key. We get him, we can turn him. He's not a soldier.

QUINLAN The United States cannot be part of a kidnapping of a foreign national. At least, not while we have a black man in the White House.

VIVIAN Oh, I'm not going to kidnap him.

QUINLAN What are you going to do then?

VIVIAN I'm going to cut his balls off and feed them to him, the two-timing bastard!

SCENE 11

LIGHTS UP ON ONE.

LAZLO AND HAND ARE SITTING BACK AT THEIR ORIGINAL TABLE, LAZLO WITH HIS BACK TO HARRY.

LAZLO I'm confused.

HARRY (TRYING TO HIDE TALKING) Uh uh.

LAZLO Whose side am I on now?

HARRY Your own.

LAZLO Good, this is good. As it has always been. (PAUSE) And what is my side doing?

HARRY This is the buy off. You give me the money, I give you the rock.

LAZLO Right, right.

HARRY You did bring the money?

LAZLO I brought the money.

HARRY Sneakers and all?

LAZLO I brought you the money. (PAUSE) You brought the rock?

HAND (BEAT) There is no rock.

LAZLO Right.

HARRY The rock never existed.

LAZLO Got it.

HARRY Okay, well, when she comes back…

ENTER VIVIAN.

VIVIAN Still here?

HARRY (RISING) I took the liberty of ordering.

VIVIAN I thought you never ate in foreign restaurants.

HARRY That's before I remembered. Before I noticed.

VIVIAN Remembered what?

MUSIC STRAINS OUT A TANGO.

HARRY They're playing our song.

HE OFFERS HER HIS HAND.

HARRY Have I told you how incredible you look? You really do. Five years since I last saw you and you don't look a day older.

VIVIAN Remembered what?

HARRY Whoever designed that dress took one look at you and got inspired. Michelangelo inspired!

VIVIAN What do you want, Harry?

HARRY It's our anniversary.

VIVIAN What are you talking about?

HARRY Our anniversary. Istanbul. Eight years to the day.

VIVIAN (PAUSE) It was Christmas, you idiot.

HARRY (UNSURE) That was Paris.

VIVIAN We've never been to Paris.

HARRY Well, don't you think we should rectify that? You, me, a cruise down the Seine.

VIVIAN Cyanide capsules under the pillow. A luger on the night stand.

HARRY Do they even make lugers anymore?

VIVIAN I was being referential.

HARRY Come on. What do you say? We can start things over. Clean slate. Put all this unpleasantness behind us. You obviously can't live without me.

VIVIAN I can't help you now.

HARRY You can't help yourself.

VIVIAN You really are full of yourself, aren't you? Let me tell you something. Let me clue you in on one or two things, shall we?

HARRY Go ahead.

VIVIAN I have absolutely no memory of sleeping with you. None. You were a mark. A source. My brief was to get close to you. I got close. The rest was just functionary.

HARRY Then, on behalf of all men who've slept with you, I'd like to applaud the tactics of Interpol. They're a beacon to law enforcement everywhere.

VIVIAN I do what I have to do.

HARRY Yes, but you didn't 'do', did you. I got away. I got away in Istanbul. I got away in Peking.

VIVIAN Shanghai.

HARRY Same thing.

VIVIAN Who says I was after you. Have some wine.

HARRY I'm not thirsty.

VIVIAN You'll need it where you're going.

HARRY Where am I going?

VIVIAN Who can tell these days. Guantanamo. Albania. I can never keep up.

HARRY You're bringing me in?

VIVIAN Consider yourself brought.

HARRY I'm curious. I mean, that is some dress. The gun is hidden exactly where?

VIVIAN I don't need a gun.

HARRY Might make a bit of a scene.

VIVIAN The waiter's CIA.

PAUSE.

HARRY I spiked the wine.

VIVIAN I poisoned the glass.

HARRY I thought you did. The escargot? Twenty milligrams of rohypnol.

VIVIAN The flowers at the other table have a chemical intoxicant.

HARRY Clever, clever. I'd have never thought of that.

VIVIAN I thought you'd try to give them to me.

HARRY Not as romantic as you thought I was then.

VIVIAN Not as smart. I love roses.

HARRY (PAUSE) There's thirty million in the bag at my feet.

VIVIAN The money is laced with a cyanide based resin. Ten minutes after handling it you'll be dead. Oh, and the zipper? Wired to a battery in the bottom, ten thousand volts.

HARRY You do seem to have thought of everything.

VIVIAN Does seem that way.

HARRY I guess I have no option but to surrender.

VIVIAN Cooperate and you'll get the very best water torture the government can afford.

HARRY You could just let me go.

VIVIAN Hmm. Tempting. Nah. Sorry.

HARRY (RISING) Well, until next time.

VIVIAN Erm, waiter?

HARRY Yeah, not so much, no.

VIVIAN You're kidding.

HARRY Look under the table. I'll wait.

VIVIAN GOES TO THE NEXT TABLE AND LOOKS UNDER AT THE SLEEPING QUINLAN.

VIVIAN Is he..?

HARRY What do you think I am? He'll be fine.

VIVIAN He drank the wine?

HARRY Lighter fluid's sleeping gas.

VIVIAN And you think I'm just going to let you walk out of here?

HARRY Yes.

VIVIAN Why?

HARRY Because, no matter how hard you try to convince yourself otherwise, you loved me. It was never going to work and we knew that, but you loved me. And you know how I know? Because I loved you. The real you. Not the smoke and mirrors, not the store front you put out whenever you think there's someone around. I loved you. And you loved me for it. And what we had, while over, while it was never going to last. It meant something. To me. It meant something. And even if it meant nothing to you, I saw you. And you know I saw you. And you know I loved you for it. And for that, if nothing else, you could never do anything to hurt me. (HE LEANS OVER AND KISSES HER ON THE CHEEK) Goodbye Vivian.

VIVIAN Harry?

HARRY STARTS TO LOOK ROCKY ON HIS FEET, THE WORLD SPINNING.

HARRY Yes.

VIVIAN You know the thing about love?

HARRY I'm… I think I need some air.

VIVIAN Feeling okay?

HARRY You… drugged…?

VIVIAN The perfume.

HARRY Oh… That's good… That's… Sneaky little…

VIVIAN You know the thing about love?

HARRY That means you…

VIVIAN HITS HIM HARD AND HE CRUMPLES TO THE FLOOR.

VIVIAN It's not nearly as satisfying as retribution.

CURTAINS.

END OF ACT 1.

ACT 2

ACT 2

SCENE 1

EIGHT MONTHS BEFORE. A HOTEL IN ISTANBUL.

LIGHTS UP. HARRY IS STANDING CENTRE STAGE, OSTENSIBLY LOOKING OUT OF A WINDOW. HE'S JUST GOTTEN UP.

WE HEAR THE SOUND OF THE CALL TO PRAYER FROM THE BLUE MOSQUE.

ENTER VIVIAN.

VIVIAN ENTERS BEHIND HARRY. DRESSED IN SWEATS, SHE LOOKS AT HIM MENACINGLY AND APPROACHES UNSEEN FROM BEHIND. SHE PUSHES A TUBE OF LIP-GLOSS INTO HIS BACK.

VIVIAN Stay exactly where you are.

HARRY You got me officer.

VIVIAN Keep your hands where I can see them.

HARRY Chanel no. 7? I'll come quietly.

HE TWISTS ROUND AND DRAWS HER INTO HIM.

VIVIAN (LOOKING OUT THE WINDOW) It's beautiful, isn't it?

HARRY Istanbul? Very. Before the smog sets in.

VIVIAN I thought you'd gone.

HARRY Coffee. It's on the table.

VIVIAN You went outside dressed like that?

HARRY Room service. Telephone is next to the coffee. For a secret agent you're a pretty deep sleeper.

VIVIAN For a conman you're something of a morning person.

HARRY Yes, you know, I like to get up, squeeze a ten mile run in before breakfast, meditate.

VIVIAN You are so full of shit.

HARRY Being full of shit is kind of what I do.

VIVIAN Is it?

HARRY Absolutely. For example. Last night? Meant nothing.

VIVIAN You were just a one night stand.

HARRY Early morning stand if you come to think about it.

VIVIAN It's all just gymnastics.

HARRY You were very cat-like.

VIVIAN It can never happen again.

HARRY God, no. Wouldn't want it to.

VIVIAN Cheap, when you come to think of it.

HARRY Tawdry.

VIVIAN Meaningless.

HARRY I don't even think I'm that good at it.

VIVIAN I'm positively frigid!

HARRY My manhood is basically non-existent.

VIVIAN You can't poke the fire with a matchstick.

HARRY Yeah, see, it's only self deprecation if you do it on yourself.

VIVIAN I like breaking the rules.

HARRY There are rules?

VIVIAN There are always rules.

HARRY Guess you'll just have to arrest me then, agent.

VIVIAN What's the charge?

HARRY I don't know. Failure to achieve satisfaction?

VIVIAN (BEAT) I could never arrest you.

HARRY Why's that?

VIVIAN Who else would I have to watch the sunrises with?

AS THE LIGHTS FALL, HAND AND QUINLAN COME ONTO THE STAGE AT A RUSH FOLLOWED SLOWLY BY LAZLO.

VIVIAN DOES NOT ACKNOWLEDGE THEM BUT AS THEY REACH HARRY HE SLUMPS INTO THEIR ARMS AND THEY DRAG HIM UP TO...

SCENE 2

SOUND OF LARGE ELECTRIC FAN.

LIGHTS UP ON A METAL CHAIR WITH LEATHER ARM AND LEG STRAPS THAT SITS CENTRE STAGE. A BATTERY AND CABLES SIT NEXT TO IT.

HAND AND LAZLO DRAG THE INERT HARRY OVER AND STRAP HIM INTO THE CHAIR.

LAZLO Make sure it is tight, yes? He is slippery character.

QUINLAN Mr. Lazlo, there really is no need for you to be here. Agent Rutledge and I…

LAZLO This is your country? No. I did not think so.

QUINLAN Interpol…

LAZLO Interpol sminterpol! This is Russia. Russia, you understand? This is not America. We do not have a line between church and police state. We have a freeway! This is Russia, and only two things matter: money and muscle. (BEAT) We're getting t-shirts. (HE LEANS OVER HARRY IN THE CHAIR) Where is my rock? Eh? What have you done with my rock? Hmm?

QUINLAN He can't hear you.

LAZLO He hears me on the inside.

HAND I think that only applies to coma patients.

LAZLO I think that only applies 'comma' to whoever I say it applies to, 'full stop'. Where is Agent Rutledge?

QUINLAN Changing. Let me be very clear on this Mr. Lazlo. You came to us. You came to the CIA and asked for our help. The CIA came to me and I came to Agent Rutledge. That's the order of things. You are here as a guest. No more. You have no jurisdiction over this interrogation whatsoever.

LAZLO You just keep thinking Butch. It's what you're good at. I take it my money will be returned?

QUINLAN Once we get the resin off. My team is cleaning it as we speak.

LAZLO The CIA are laundering my money for me now, eh? This will make a great story for Oprah.

QUINLAN (PAUSE) You're not really going on Oprah?

LAZLO I know, it's good, isn't it! Once the deal with the Cubans has gone through. I give her car, live, what you think?

QUINLAN I think you should jump up and down on the sofa.

LAZLO Man, I love American TV. This is where I learn my English, you see? As a little boy. I learn everything from movies. Butch Cassidy, James Bond, these were my teachers. Topov.

QUINLAN Topov?

LAZLO Fiddler On The Roof! You know this? Great American movie. All time.

QUINLAN It's set in Russia!

LAZLO Trust me, it's American movie. (SINGING) If I were a rich man! Learn all my English from that. Faktish!

ENTER VIVIAN.

DRESSED IN THE SAME SWEATS AS THE PREVIOUS SCENE, SHE IS DRYING HER HAIR WITH A TOWEL.

VIVIAN Why haven't you started the interrogation?

HAND We used up all the smelling salts on Agent Quinlan.

QUINLAN What kind of con man uses sleeping gas.

LAZLO A smart one.

VIVIAN LOOKS AT HARRY CLOSELY.

VIVIAN He's awake.

QUINLAN He'll be out for hours.

LAZLO He is sleeping like baby.

VIVIAN Trust me, he's awake.

THE THREE TURN TO LOOK AT HIM.

HARRY Okay. Which one of you perverts removed my clothes?

HAND HITS HIM CASUALLY, KNOCKING HIM OVER.

VIVIAN Hey, hey! There'll be none of that! You hear me? He's no good to us with a concussion, understand. (TO QUINLAN) Pick him up.

HARRY You hit like a girl. A really well built girl who's being forced to take gender determination tests by the Olympic Committee, but a girl, nonetheless.

VIVIAN Where's the rock, Lime?

HARRY Where's the soul, Agent Rutledge?

VIVIAN We know it wasn't with you in the restaurant. We know it isn't at your hotel. Yes, we know where you are staying. It wasn't even at your apartment in Marseilles. So…

HARRY (TO LAZLO) Listen to me Victor.

QUINLAN Victor ain't gonna help you.

HARRY They don't care about you. They don't care about the rock. They only care that you don't have it, you understand me? I knew they were on to me. I knew she'd be at the... I'm a... I'm a business man, Victor. I stole something off you fair and square. Straight down the line. Deals still on. But the price just went up. Double.

QUINLAN HITS HIM SENDING HIM THE OTHER WAY.

QUINLAN Goddamn cocksucker!

VIVIAN Hey! What the hell is wrong with you?! Think he can talk with his jaw wired shut?

QUINLAN Arrogant little cocksucker!

HARRY Ask yourself why they're here, Victor? Ask yourself what's in it for them! Why would the CIA risk kidnapping a British national...

QUINLAN You're a scumbag! No one cares about you!

HARRY Get me out of this, Victor. Get me out and I'll tell you exactly what the rock does!

QUINLAN LAUNCHES HIMSELF TOWARDS HARRY.

QUINLAN You goddamn cocksucker! I'm going to knock the teeth right out of your head!

VIVIAN (RESTRAINING HIM) Quinlan! Quinlan! Dammit! (SHE GETS HIM UNDER CONTROL) Agent Quinlan outside! Now!

QUINLAN Jesus! Fine. Fine. I'm fine.

VIVIAN Outside now!

QUINLAN Fine. (TO THE GROUP) We're right outside. You understand me? We're right outside and we can hear everything you say. Got it!

VIVIAN Agent! Now, if you don't mind.

EXIT VIVIAN AND QUINLAN.

SCENE 3

ENTER ANNA.

READS INTO A VOICE RECORDER.

ANNA   In July two thousand and nine, a Maltese flagged cargo vessel carrying one point eight million dollars worth of wood disappeared in the Arctic sea. When it was recovered almost a month later, eight Estonians were charged with pirating and the FSB investigating the matter considered the case closed. Why Johnny Depp and his friends would be hiding out in the Arctic Sea of all places was never questioned. Why they would attempt to steal wood, a relatively minor cargo for that shipping lane, was apparently only a question a woodchuck could answer. Despite persistent rumours of arms deals by the Russian military to embargoed countries and the involvement of Mossad in preventing the ship from reaching its preferred destination of Algeria, the case was considered closed by almost everyone. (BEAT) Except Mikhail Voitenko, editor of the maritime online magazine, Sovfracht. Volitenko, who was among the first to cast doubt on official explanations about the ship's disappearance, fled Moscow in September after death threats and fear of arrest from the state police over his continued questioning of the…

SCENE 4

AS SCENE 2.

HARRY You're sure they can't hear us?

LAZLO Mr. Hand has a noisy white machine.

HAND A white noise machine.

LAZLO He is a fachman when it comes to the electronics. They cannot hear.

HARRY (TO HAND) You might want to actually try pulling your punches next time.

HAND You said to make it realistic.

HARRY I asked you for thirty million and you brought me gym clothes. I thought the standard still applied.

LAZLO It is going good, yes?

HARRY Apart from the hitting bits.

LAZLO They really think you have the rock!

HARRY They really think I have the rock.

LAZLO Two days. Can you believe it? Two days since they intercepted anything! Mr. Hand and I, last night we held a one hour conversation saying we start a new Al Qaeda cell and blow up the Eiffel Tower. Very convincing. And nothing! Can you believe it?

HARRY That he can speak for up to an hour? Not really.

LAZLO I would not have believed it. Yes? That you, a total, and I hope you don't take this the wrong way or anything, I like you, but a total loser, would have the balls to con the world's intelligence community. You have quite the cojones eh? Eh? This is better than Rocky III, I tell you.

HARRY Alright, so just get me out of the chair and we'll…

LAZLO Ah. That. I don't think so.

HARRY Victor…

LAZLO No, they need to torture you. These people. They train. You cannot deprive them of the practice.

HARRY Victor…

LAZLO No, no. You stay, we go. (TO HAND) We go.

ENTER ANNA.

ANNA IS LEAVING THE HOUSE. SHE CHECKS HER KEYS,

HER BAG.

HARRY Victor, listen. It doesn't work. They have to think you got the rock back. They have to think you accepted the deal, that now you know what it's worth.

LAZLO I know what it's worth.

HARRY What?

LAZLO Your life!

HARRY Don't be stupid. Victor, listen, this is what got you in trouble in the first place. All those journalists?

LAZLO Journalists?

ANNA MOVES TO LEAVE. HAND APPEARS AND SHOOTS HER IN THE HEAD.

LIGHTS DOWN ON ANNA AND HAND.

HARRY Why do you think the intelligence agencies are spying on you in the first place? You shot that journalist. Right on her doorstep.

LAZLO What do CIA care for a Russian journalist?

HARRY Free speech is the first amendment.

LAZLO It's amendment! If they really cared about it they'd put it in the original!

HARRY If they don't think you have the rock…

LAZLO But I do have the rock.

HARRY What rock?

LAZLO (PULLING A ROCK OUT OF HIS POCKET) This one!

HARRY (PAUSE) What the hell is that?

LAZLO I don't know. My wife got it at a modern art festival. Hideous isn't it. Sometimes I think she has no taste. Still, good head. It is a man-made, or something. Synthetic. Only one like it in the world.

HARRY You can't possibly try passing that off as the real one!

LAZLO Why not? They know nothing! Anyway, that wicked-pedia

page you made on the rock? The one the CIA are using to base their intelligence off? Mr. Hand put picture of this on there last night. For them, this IS the rock.

HARRY You can't possibly think they'll believe you.

LAZLO Believe me? Why not. They believe you, and you are pole-smoking cock-sucker schulik. I am respected business man. And now they have tape. Tape of you, thrashing around in your little chair. While in my hands, I have a very singular looking piece of rock. The evidence does not lie.

HARRY Actually, they'll probably just shoot you and take the rock.

SCENE 5

LIGHTS ON VIVIAN AND QUINLAN.

OUTSIDE THE INTERROGATION ROOM. THEIR DEMEANOUR IS AT FIRST ANTAGONISTIC BUT QUICKLY FADES TO CALM ONCE THEY KNOW THEY'RE NOT BEING WATCHED.

VIVIAN Get in there!

QUINLAN (RUNNING, THEN PAUSING TO SMOKE A CIGARETTE) It's going well.

VIVIAN You think it's safe to leave them in there together?

QUINLAN If they're in it together, why not? If not, who knows, maybe he'll shoot him.

VIVIAN How's it coming with Echelon?

QUINLAN The bank accounts? (HE PULLS OUT A SMALL TABLET DEVICE) Here, see for yourself.

VIVIAN STEPS AWAY AND SURREPTITIOUSLY PLUGS SOMETHING INTO THE DEVICE.

VIVIAN This is all of them.

QUINLAN Near as we can tell. Thirty million was paid out of the Caymans last week. Two days before the robbery. Looks like you were right. It's a set up.

VIVIAN At the moment that's all it does. Looks like it.

QUINLAN Sometimes they are just the jedi you're looking for.

VIVIAN Have we pulled surveillance?

QUINLAN Can't have him crashing satellites down on us. You done?

HE TAKES THE DEVICE BACK.

VIVIAN I thought I was going to be the bad cop.

QUINLAN Thought I'd save you the effort.

VIVIAN What's that supposed to mean?

QUINLAN You figure it out.

VIVIAN He was a mark. Nothing more.

QUINLAN Yeah, okay.

VIVIAN We used him to get close to Kirmanov. Nothing more.

QUINLAN Yeah, you know, except. That's bullshit. I've read the file. You were never interested in Kirmanov.

VIVIAN Kirmanov…

QUINLAN You became interested in Kirmanov after you hooked up with Lime. After. Not before.

VIVIAN What are you talk…

QUINLAN You know what? It's okay. Screw it. My job at the restaurant was to make sure you brought Lime in. You brought Lime in. Why should I give a shit about the hows and whys. You did your job. The rest, I don't care. You know what I was doing five days ago? I was breaking up a terror cell. Not a "I feel like burning the flag" kind of terrorist cell. Not a "let's get some stupid piece of rock that stops Echelon from working" piece of crap which, you know, is, yes, important and everything, but an honest-to-god, semtex and AK47 type terror cell. The kind of terror cell that affects real people's lives, that kills real people. So, yes, this is important and everything, but don't expect me to get all teary eyed at the prospect of some Russian mobster offing a piece of shit conman over a thing that will affect, no one; that is cared about by, no one. Screw it. You want to play bad cop, knock yourself out. But why should you? Why should you have to? It was a relationship, it wasn't a relationship. He was a mark, he wasn't a mark. It doesn't matter! Why should you have to? He dumped you. You want a little payback? Go fuck yourself. Get your head back in the game.

VIVIAN Are you done?

QUINLAN I'm done.

VIVIAN He didn't dump me.

QUINLAN Sure he did.

VIVIAN He did NOT dump me.

QUINLAN You want to know who's won the fight? You look for the guy still standing.

VIVIAN What the hell has that got to do with what happened between us?

QUINLAN (SHRUGGING) You're the one who's still cut up about it.

EXIT QUINLAN.

SCENE 6

HARRY ENTERS BEHIND VIVIAN, DRESSED AS BEFORE.

HARRY Have you seen my shirt?

VIVIAN Hmm?

HARRY My shirt, have you seen it.

VIVIAN It's where you left it last night.

HARRY Cunning. Why didn't I think of that. (HE LOOKS AROUND THE ROOM. VIVIAN WATCHES HIM PASSIVELY.) You still here tonight?

VIVIAN Sorry?

HARRY Are you still in town tonight?

VIVIAN Why do you ask?

HARRY I want to see you. Seriously, you haven't seen my shirt?

VIVIAN I don't know about tonight.

HARRY Okay.

VIVIAN I cannot just drop everything whenever you want.

HARRY I don't expect you to.

VIVIAN It sounded like you did.

HARRY I'm late. Why are you trying to pick a fight with me?

VIVIAN Where is all your money?

HARRY I'm sorry?

HARRY HAS FOUND A SHIRT. HE STARTS TO PUT IT ON, NOT NOTICING A STAIN.

VIVIAN Where is all your money? On the Istanbul thing alone, how much money did you make?

HARRY Seriously? After expenses? Bragging rights. You've no idea how much satellite images cost these days.

VIVIAN And this?

HARRY I have means. What is this about? (HE NOTICES THE STAIN) Shit. Seriously, I am so late.

VIVIAN For Lazlo.

HARRY Yes, for Lazlo. What is this about?

VIVIAN He's not coming.

HARRY What do you mean he's not coming?

VIVIAN He got a tip off.

PAUSE.

HARRY What are you saying Vivian?

VIVIAN (SUDDENLY BUSY) The deal is off. You need to leave Moscow.

HARRY He got a tip off?

VIVIAN It was a stupid plan.

HARRY It was… So, what you're really saying is, you tipped him off.

VIVIAN Yes.

HARRY You, Interpol, or you, you?

VIVIAN Does it matter?

HARRY To me? Absolutely.

VIVIAN It was a stupid plan.

HARRY Damn it! Interpol? So, he gets a free pass? Is that it? A free pass from Interpol. The guy's an international arms dealer and he gets a free pass?

VIVIAN Oh, like you give a shit about anything like that!

HARRY You've had enough on him for months, months! You could have arrested him anytime you liked, but you didn't, and why? Government ties? Oil ties? That doesn't bother you?

VIVIAN He's a mark! A mark! You're a god-damned conman. You don't care about anything like that.

HARRY But you're supposed to! Litvinenko, what about him?

VIVIAN What about him?

HARRY If they know this is a set up, what do you think they'll do to him?

VIVIAN Litvinenko's a big boy.

PAUSE.

HARRY You were trying to pick a fight with me.

VIVIAN What?

HARRY Before. You were trying to pick a fight with me. What was that?

VIVIAN What does it matter?

HARRY You just shopped me to Interpol.

VIVIAN They knew about it already.

HARRY They knew about it already?

VIVIAN Why do you think I'm here?

HARRY Well, that's just wonderful, isn't it. That's just peachy! Eight months of hard work down the drain! Why aren't I under arrest?

VIVIAN What?

HARRY Arrest me? If that's what you're here for, arrest me!

VIVIAN I don't want to talk about this.

HARRY They're just letting him walk. Lazlo. You're letting them walk.

VIVIAN Do not internalize this. Do not make it into one of your little stories. This is not a story, you understand? It is my job. Interpol knew. It's not about you and me, it's not! They knew. Outside! From Litvinenko. They knew! This is what it is. Not everything is a neat little bow. Not everything is a story you are trying to tell. You understand? Life is messy, and that's what this is! If I was telling them, do you think you would be here? You think you would not be dead in the snow out there? This is what it is!

HARRY And us, are we what we are?

VIVIAN Nothing is what it seems, you taught me that.

SCENE 7

AS BEFORE. HARRY IN HIS SEAT, LAZLO AND HAND NEAR HIM.

ENTER QUINLAN.

LAZLO Ah, Agent Quinlan. We were wondering where you'd got to. We are eager for the fun to start, are we not, Mr. Hand?

QUINLAN Save it for someone who cares, Lazlo.

LAZLO Really? This is not the 'come hither' eyes I have come to expect from the CIA.

HARRY Could you guys hurry it along. I've got a date.

QUINLAN You know the thing with shooting someone. It itches. Not in the conventional sense I'll grant you. But in the brain. Right where you can't get to it. You think it's nothing, think it's gone and then, woop, there it is again! Kind of like the feelings you have for an ex-girlfriend.

LAZLO All very fascinating, I'm sure. But…

QUINLAN As a rule. I don't like to shoot people. I don't like to date, either. Dating's a mistake. It'll give you the itch, but shooting's something you want to avoid at all costs.

HAND I don't…

QUINLAN Still, when it comes to national security.

LAZLO I am a person of great interest to the United States.

QUINLAN Yes you are, yes you are. Right up until you're not. And you know how you change sides? You stop being in our best interests. You have something, say, a rock. A rock that can do untold damage to the United States; well, anyone who had that rock, doesn't matter if they're a friend or not. Doesn't matter if they are. They have that rock they can sell it to whoever they like and who they like might be people who are not in the United States' best interests. You catch my drift?

HARRY I did warn you.

HAND Wait; you are saying that this rock is a threat to the United States?

QUINLAN (PAUSE) Alright, ten points to you. My bad. Still, person who had that rock, I could just shoot in the head. Right then and there.

LAZLO If you shoot me, Agent Quinlan, you will be in a great deal of trouble.

QUINLAN If I shoot you they'll throw me a ticker tape parade down Main Street. Now give me the goddamn rock!

HARRY Uh oh.

LAZLO What rock?

QUINLAN The rock in that pocket.

LAZLO Oh, that rock! Sure, sure. Have it! It's my wife's.

HAND It's a present for Agent Vivian.

QUINLAN Sorry.

HAND (TO HAND) Oh, yes, very good. (TO QUINLAN) It's quartz. Man made.

ENTER VIVIAN.

VIVIAN What the hell is going on here?

LAZLO Mr. Quinlan was just showing us his interrogation techniques. (TAKING THE ROCK FROM QUINLAN) Here, for you! It matches the colour of your hostility towards men.

HARRY Seriously. I bought flowers and everything.

LAZLO Mr. Hand and I will, I think, get some fresh air. The sight of blood… Actually, the sight of blood gives me enormous boner, but Mr. Hand is quite the schwach. Mr. Hand?

EXIT LAZLO AND HAND.

QUINLAN GOES ACROSS TO THE BATTERY AND STARTS TO CONNECT THE JUMPERS TO HARRY.

HARRY So, this is how it's going to be is it.

QUINLAN This is how it's going to be.

HARRY Quick bit of electrocution before we move on to the water-boarding. Maybe get some Marines to take humiliating photos with me. I have to warn you, I look good in a hood.

QUINLAN Tell us where the rock is and we won't have to.

HARRY I don't know what you're talking about.

QUINLAN Listen. We know you know. We know you know we know. You know, that we know, that you know we know. So why don't we all just save some time here and tell us where the rock is.

HARRY (PAUSE) Okay, well, seeing as we're all in the know…

QUINLAN Where's the rock.

HARRY As far as I know, the Rock, right now, is shooting a movie in Hollywood. Okay, it's not acting, acting but his wrestling background does give him a versatility that bridges humour and action in way few others are capable of.

QUINLAN (TO VIVIAN) Does he ever just shut up?

VIVIAN Not that I've noticed.

QUINLAN Give us the rock and we can all go home. Well, not you, you're going to a Russian gulag but if you tell us now, we won't torture you on the way there. Sound fair?

HARRY That's what it's come to, is it? The combined might of the American and European intelligence agencies at the bidding of a Russian mobster. What next? Mossad working with the PLO?

QUINLAN (SHOUTING) Where's the rock?

HARRY I don't know what you're talking about.

QUINLAN Where's the rock?

HARRY Go, and I say this with a great amount of affection, fuck yourself!

QUINLAN Give us the rock!

HARRY Or what? You're going to torture me anyway!

QUINLAN Torture you?

HARRY That is what you said.

QUINLAN Oh, I'm not going to torture you.

VIVIAN You're not?

HARRY You're not?

QUINLAN The United States does not engage in the torture of prisoners. (BEAT) I'm pretty sure about that. Wait, yes, there was a memo. (BEAT) The United States is opposed to torture in all forms. I cannot torture a prisoner under my command.

HARRY Well, that is a relief.

QUINLAN (TURNING TO VIVIAN) Torture the prisoner under my command. I'll be outside.

EXIT QUINLAN.

VIVIAN AND HARRY LOOK AT EACH OTHER.

HARRY How's this going for you?

VIVIAN Not exactly living up to billing.

HARRY You can say that again.

VIVIAN Lazlo double crossed you?

HARRY Who'd have thought?

VIVIAN So.

HARRY Do me a favour, get these electrodes off, would you? I think there's a residual current.

VIVIAN (GOING OVER TO THE BATTERY) Who'd you have at the apartment?

HARRY Sorry?

VIVIAN You had women at the apartment.

HARRY You have to be kidding me.

VIVIAN Not at all.

HARRY You've been seeing Davis!

VIVIAN I had to see Davis! It was the only way I could make sure I got the case. (SHE PUTS HER HAND ON THE DIAL) There were condoms all over the floor?

HARRY So?

VIVIAN TURNS THE DIAL MOMENTARILY AND HARRY JERKS. IT'S NOT REALLY PAINFUL.

HARRY (CONT.) Ow, hey, stop screwing around with that.

VIVIAN You couldn't have gone to a hotel?

HARRY Where would the fun be in that?

VIVIAN TURNS THE DIAL FURTHER UP THIS TIME.

HARRY Jesus! Hey, that actually hurts, you know what I mean? That could cause actual brain damage!

VIVIAN (ANGRY) Right there, on the floor. Like the pig that you are!

HARRY Baby, sweetheart, there was no one! I was just trying to, you know, make you jealous. Hand to God! You were seeing Davis and… Wait, wait! Sweetheart, think about it. Let's not blow this all out of proportion!

VIVIAN LEAVES IT ON WHILE TALKING.

VIVIAN Every time I came there! And I had to see that!? Every time!

HARRY (OUT OF BREATH AND CLEARLY IN PAIN) Sweetheart, not to, you know, or anything, but (BEAT) you left me.

VIVIAN GOES TO TURN IT UP AGAIN.

SCENE 8

LAZLO AND HAND ARE TALKING.

LAZLO Farkakt.

HAND Exactly.

LAZLO What can we do?

HAND They will not be happy.

LAZLO I know they will not be happy. This I know.

HAND Assurances were made.

LAZLO Yes, yes.

HAND You promised them that you could provide a no-fly zone over South Ossetia next summer in return for…

LAZLO I know what was promised. You do not have to remind me.

HAND Assurances were made.

LAZLO Listen, you work for me, alright? You keep thinking about the big picture, yes? And to you, I am the big picture, you catch my drift.

HAND And when you are gone? To your new life? You made them assurances. You told them that if they let you go you would deliver them Eschelon. You would deliver South Ossetia.

LAZLO And I have!

HAND The key to Russia is the oil. Only with oil can Russia once more be great! Communism fell to greed. Democracy fell to greed. Russia needs oil. It needs control of the pipelines so that it can sell to China and for that, it needs little hill towns like South Ossetia. To be great again, this is what we must do! If we are to feed our people, this is what we must do! The West; they spy, they sanction, they tie us up in bureaucracy in the UN. This is what they want. Incrementally, piece by piece! What they cannot take, they delay, they delay until their own deals are in place. And if these journalists...

LAZLO Hey, the journalists were not my idea! Alexander, okay, who was to know. But this Anna Korenka!? This is too much. It is too much! Too much spotlight.

HAND   Assurances were made.

LAZLO Assurances were made! Stop saying that. Assurances were fulfilled! Assurances are being assured, are they not? Every man speaks under torture! He will tell them about the rock. They will think I have the rock, which means they think Russia has the rock, and they will remove their surveillance before it is compromised. Assurances are being assured!

HAND   And if he tells them there is no rock?

LAZLO Then they won't believe him. He is thief.

HAND   This is not going to be enough.

LAZLO (SIGHING) Yes, yes. Alright. Have it your own way. I was just starting to like him as well.

ENTER QUINLAN.

LAZLO Ah, Agent Quinlan! Has Mr. Lime told you the whereabouts of my property yet, hmm?

QUINLAN   Agent Rutledge is getting it out of him now.

LAZLO Yes, I'm sure she is.

HAND PUTS A HAND ON LAZLO'S SHOULDER.

LAZLO (CONT.) Right. Yes. Erm (TO QUINLAN) Perhaps Mr. Hand should supervise, yes? He has... expertise in this department.

QUINLAN   Knock yourself out. Better yet, knock him out.

EXIT HAND.

LAZLO (OFFERING A CIGARETTE) Smoke?

QUINLAN   I quit.

LAZLO Humph. Me too. (THE TWO STAND IN SILENCE) You know, I never understood the fascination with this whole non-smoking thing these days. My wife, she quit. She had this book; it was supposed to help her stop. Lots of facts about smoking, that kind of thing. It had this chapter; breaking the myth. Oy! It says; living long is not better than living well. And then say; yes, but, is better to die young of horrible disease than live long? What is this? Live long, don't live long. Better not to die of horrible disease at all, I think. I ask you this, you made love to good looking woman? (HE LOOKS AT QUINLAN) Okay, you made love to 'okay' looking woman? Yes? Okay. Well, I ask you this. Better to make love to love to one wonderful, perfect woman for one night? One night! But one night you can remember (HE TAPS HIS HEAD) here and, you know, use memory of later, or make love to hundreds of really ugly women with bad smell? Eh? Eh? You take the one woman. Me too. (PAUSE) You have had woman, yes?

LIGHTS UP ON HARRY IN THE CHAIR. HAND ENTERS.

HAND   Baba s vosu kobyle legche. Where is Agent Rutledge?

LAZLO Of course. I have had hundreds of 'beautiful' women. But you know, analogy is analogy.

HARRY She stepped out for some fresh air.

QUINLAN Must be nice being rich.

LAZLO Meh, it has its plus points.

HAND   What did you tell her?

HARRY About the rock? Nothing. But she got my grandmother's secret ingredient for Yorkshire pudding, damn her.

QUINLAN What's with the Yiddish, by the way. Since we're talking?

HAND You told her nothing?

HAND MOVES TO PICK UP A WEAPON. HARRY WATCHES HIM.

LAZLO My grandmother is Jewish. You know this? Jewish-ism is on the mother's side, like Oedipus.

HARRY You mean, did 'I' betray 'you'. Not yet.

LAZLO I did not know this of course, this she kept hidden. Obvious reasons. Now, she lives on the Mount of Olives. Go figure.

HAND APPROACHES HARRY WITH THE WEAPON. LIGHTS FADE ON LAZLO AND QUINLAN.

HARRY This doesn't have to go this way. Sixty million and the deal's good. There's no need for bloodshed.

HAND (PAUSE) No… I do not have joke. Nothing. (SHRUGS) Life is not fun.

HAND AND HARRY FIGHT, WITH HARRY REMAINING TIED TO THE CHAIR. IN CONTRAST TO EARLIER HOWEVER, HARRY PROVES TO BE AN EXPERT FIGHTER AND, WITHOUT LEAVING THE CHAIR, KILLS HAND.

LIGHTS SLOW FADE ON THEM.

LIGHTS UP ON LAZLO AND QUINLAN. BOTH ARE SMOKING.

QUINLAN (LOOKING AT THE CIGARETTE) I'd say I'd forgotten but it's more like forgotten to remember, if you know what I mean.

LAZLO See! It's good. What makes you feel good is good.

QUINLAN Guess I'm just weak willed.

LAZLO Takes as much to quit as to carry on. (PAUSE) Okay, I can't back that up. Feeling good is power. Yes? You feel good, you feel powerful. You feel powerful, you do, yes?

QUINLAN I thought money is power.

LAZLO Only if it makes you feel good.

QUINLAN Thirty million is a lot of money.

LAZLO Is it? (BEAT) Yes, I suppose it is.

QUINLAN DRAWS HIS GUN.

QUINLAN You know, I've never really shot anyone. No one. All that before, about how it feels to kill a man. Total bullshit. Fifteen years in the service and never even had to draw my weapon. Can you believe that?

LAZLO I count you luck man then.

QUINLAN What's it feel like?

LAZLO What?

QUINLAN To shoot someone.

LAZLO I'm businessman. How would I know?

QUINLAN Yeah, but you've had people killed.

LAZLO Is not the same. You order hotdog you don't think about the pig. Everyone kills people. Every day. You buy diamond, you think people don't die in the mine? To get your diamond? You buy house, you don't care if someone fall off ladder building it. To you, was worth it! No one cares.

QUINLAN It doesn't get to you?

LAZLO (SHRUGS) Why should it?

QUINLAN Thirty million is a lot of money.

HE SHOOTS LAZLO IN THE STOMACH. LAZLO LOOKS UP AT HIM IN SURPRISE.

QUINLAN (CONT., IN EXPLANATION) Weak willed.

HE SHOOTS HIM AGAIN AND LAZLO FALLS DOWN, PRESUMED DEAD.

LIGHTS DOWN ON THEM.

SCENE 9

VIVIAN STANDS CENTRE STAGE, LOOKING INTO THE DISTANCE. SHE SEEMS ANGRY, FRUSTRATED. IN HER HAND SHE HOLDS A NEWSPAPER.

ENTER HARRY.

HARRY, FULLY DRESSED ENTERS, HE'S CARRYING A BOTTLE OF CHAMPAGNE. AND HAS THE OPPOSITE DEMEANOUR, HAPPY AND EXCITED.

HARRY Great. You're already here. (HE SEES HER MOOD) I know, I know, I'm late. I'm sorry. Look, champagne! The deal took longer than I thought and then the Bakerloo line was closed so there's not a cab to be found. (HE STARTS TO UNDRESS) Did you get my message. Hi. Hi. I'm sorry, really, it was completely beyond my control. And then there was this whole thing with the concierge and… Anyway, I'm here now and, wow, you look fantastic. You really do. Honey? Sweetheart? Look, I'm sorry, the Bakerloo line? Not my fault? Bollinger '87? No? Really? It's just that. Don't get me wrong, I liked the mail. I loved the mail, but my flight is in a couple of hours and if we're going to… Honey? Flight? Couple of hours? Sex? (HE RELAXES AND GOES TO HER) Hey, I'm sorry. Seriously. God, you look good. Smell good too! You'd never think it but sitting around a gentleman's club for nine hours with eighty year old fascists can make you incredibly horny.

VIVIAN (PUSHING HIM OFF) They killed him.

HARRY Who?

VIVIAN Litvinenko.

HARRY Yeah. He was sick. Cancer.

VIVIAN No. They poisoned him.

HARRY Who did?

VIVIAN The… I don't know. The Russian mafia, the government. Whatever the difference is these days.

HARRY When?

VIVIAN Now. Today.

HARRY Really?

VIVIAN It's in the god-damned newspaper.

HARRY That's terrible. (PAUSE) So, email. Sex!

VIVIAN Is that all you've got to say about it.

HARRY I don't know. Is anything I can say going to move this conversation into the bedroom because I've got this flight…

VIVIAN They have to be stopped.

HARRY We could do it out here I suppose. The table looks sturdy enough.

VIVIAN That's all you can think about? Sex?

HARRY Sex and death honey and well, you sent the email…

VIVIAN It was Lazlo

HARRY Of course it was Lazlo.

VIVIAN Lazlo and Kermanov.

HARRY It's terrible.

VIVIAN They have to be stopped.

HARRY Right. Totally. Now, getting back to the email…

VIVIAN I spoke to Davis. Nothing. I phoned Lyon directly and got his god-damned answering machine.

HARRY (LOOKING AT THE EMAIL) See, it says: "At the Highbury. Stop. Red panties, stop. Need you to never, never, never… stop." And I applaud the anachronisms.

VIVIAN What the hell are you talking about?! He was your friend.

HARRY (SIGHING) He was a mark. A tool. I used him to get the story out I needed to get out. But, yes I liked him, and, if it happened…

VIVIAN What do you mean 'if it happened'?

HARRY If they killed him, it's a tragedy. And someone, oh, I don't know, Interpol perhaps, should do something about it but I haven't seen you in three weeks and there was this whole promise of red panties and… (HE FOLDS) Fine. Go to Davis again. Go to Lyon!

VIVIAN I told you, he's not answering.

HARRY Of course he's not answering. You basically gave Lazlo a golden pass three months ago. Him, the mafia, you're never going after them and you know it. You had your chance to take them down. You didn't.

VIVIAN I'll go public.

HARRY You can't.

VIVIAN Why not.

HARRY Well, for one, you're a spy. It's hardly overt. But two, you signed I don't know how many official secrets acts. You go public, you go to jail. If they don't kill you first.

VIVIAN You go public then. You know as much…

HARRY More.

VIVIAN …more than me, anyway.

HARRY Who'd believe me?

VIVIAN Damn it. They killed him! A journalist and we put him in that situation. We gave him the story! And they killed him!

HARRY Why do we always have conversations when I'm half dressed?

VIVIAN I'm not joking around.

HARRY Alright. You want the truth. Still, now, you could arrest these guys whenever you want. Murdering a journalist? That's small fry. Arms trafficking. Sex slavery. Mass murder. Echelon's got tons on these guys but you'll never use it. Why? Because like it or not these guys are the face of capitalism in Russia and you guys need the capital.

VIVIAN I'll go deep throat. Reveal everything.

HARRY Well, as sexy as that sounds, you can't.

VIVIAN Why not?

HARRY They just killed one journalist. Why not another? Talk to anyone and you're signing a death warrant.

VIVIAN You could do it.

HARRY I don't think so.

VIVIAN You said it yourself, he's never met you! Lazlo, face to face, you could…

HARRY No.

VIVIAN Listen to me. You. Me. With everything we know. With everything we've done. We can't let them get away with it. You can't let them get away with it! I can't believe you're just going to let them win on this!

HARRY Nice try. But I didn't let them win. I let you win.

(PAUSE)

VIVIAN So, how do we do it. Teach me.

HARRY Get the information out there?

VIVIAN Fry them! Come on. You must know a way!?

HARRY (PAUSE) A fake journalist would do it, I suppose.

VIVIAN A fake journalist.

HARRY Set up some fake IDs, rent an apartment. Create a paper trail. Start online obviously but with just enough to get the papers, the magazines interested. It's simple enough. No one to kill. No way to find who's writing the articles.

VIVIAN And we write them?

HARRY We?

VIVIAN Absolutely! With what we know. Together. This whole

thing! We can blow them out of the water!

HARRY We?

VIVIAN We? We? What? Is there a toilet in here? We do this! We are responsible! We! You and I. We do this. Together. And no one will ever know!

HARRY I don't know.

VIVIAN You said it yourself. Set up a fake journalist. Where?

HARRY Russia. It would have to be Russia.

VIVIAN Everything you know, everything I know. We leak it all, to the press. Through the fake journalist!

HARRY All this to ease your conscience?

VIVIAN What do you mean?

HARRY Well, at the risk of spoiling the sex…

VIVIAN Screw the sex.

HARRY Oh, honey, what do you think I've been trying to do!? At the risk of spoiling the sex… You feel guilty. If you hadn't tipped off Lazlo then both he and his friends would be rotting in some Balkan jail right now. Penniless. As it is, they're free, walking around and killing the very journalists who were supposed to be putting them there. You're guilty and you're acting out.

VIVIAN How dare you!

HARRY Look…

VIVIAN No, you listen to me, Harry. You do not get to lecture to me about morality. Alright? You are not Robin Hood. You steal from people and use the money to buy this!

HARRY Yes, but I'm not the one who has trouble sleeping through the night.

SHE SLAPS HIM.

VIVIAN You are going to help me do this. You are going to help me set up this fake journalist and you are going to help me bring these bastards down or, I swear to god, I will shoot you resisting arrest.

EXIT VIVIAN.

HARRY I suppose a quickie's out of the question then?

FADE TO BLACK.

SCENE 10

HARRY IS BACK IN HIS CHAIR, HAND STILL DEAD AT HIS FEET.

QUINLAN ENTERS.

HARRY Hi. (IN EXPLANATION) He slipped.

QUINLAN DRAWS HIS GUN AND APPROACHES HARRY CAREFULLY.

QUINLAN What happened here?

HARRY Torture really takes it out of you.

QUINLAN Is he dead?

HARRY That's one way of looking at it.

QUINLAN What's another?

HARRY Okay, that's the only way to look at it.

QUINLAN (AIMING THE GUN) Well, that's practically resisting arrest, isn't it.

HARRY You're just going to shoot me?

QUINLAN That is the plan, yes.

HARRY What will that gain you?

QUINLAN (PAUSE) Good point.

(HE TURNS THE GUN AROUND AND SMACKS IT ACROSS HARRY'S FACE VICIOUSLY.)

HARRY What the hell?

QUINLAN Where's the thirty million?

HARRY What?

QUINLAN HITS HIM AGAIN.

QUINLAN Where's the thirty million?

HARRY You've got to be kidding me!?

QUINLAN HITS HIM AGAIN.

QUINLAN Does it feel like I'm kidding?

HARRY What is it with you guys? Are there no honest men left anymore?

QUINLAN HITS HIM AGAIN.

QUINLAN Where's the money?

HARRY (STARTING TO LAUGH) I... oh, god.

QUINLAN This is funny?

HARRY You have no idea!

QUINLAN Tell me where the thirty million is.

HARRY What thirty million?

QUINLAN HITS HIM AGAIN.

QUINLAN I've seen his bank accounts!

HARRY Whose?

QUINLAN Lazlo's!

HARRY (CHANGING DEMEANOUR) You've accessed his bank accounts?

QUINLAN Through Echelon. Sure.

HARRY Then it's too late.

QUINLAN I know he paid you thirty million. I know you're working together. I don't give a damn. I just want the money!

HARRY Then you're as out of luck as you are stupid. There is no money. He didn't pay me squat!

QUINLAN Bullshit!

HARRY Believe what you want.

QUINLAN Thirty million is missing from his bank account!

HARRY How the hell would I know? Maybe he bought his wife a new yacht.

QUINLAN HITS HIM AGAIN.

QUINLAN You will tell me. Not even your Uncle Felix can help you now?

HARRY Who?

QUINLAN (MOTIONING) I know everything about you. I know all about your Uncle Felix and his…

HARRY My Uncle who? Felix was the cat!

QUINLAN STANDS BACK, THINKING. HE PULLS OUT THE GADGET FROM BEFORE AND CLICKS IT ON.

QUINLAN Give me the money!

HARRY And what, you'll shoot me.

QUINLAN Oh, I'm going to shoot you. But give me the money and I won't shoot her.

VIVIAN ENTERS UNSEEN AND DRAWS HER GUN, APPROACHING UNSEEN BEHIND QUINLAN.

HARRY (MOTIONING TO THE DEVICE) They're empty aren't they? Lazlo's bank accounts. What did you do with him? Kill him?

QUINLAN She put a program into Echelon. Used it to access his bank accounts.

HARRY That was the plan, yes.

QUINLAN This whole thing. This was the idea from the beginning wasn't it?

VIVIAN Apart from shooting an unarmed man in cold blood, yes. Put the gun down.

QUINLAN How much was there?

HARRY Little over a billion, give or take.

VIVIAN Put the gun down!

QUINLAN All of it. You took all his money?

HARRY Every red cent.

QUINLAN Why?

VIVIAN Put the gun down now!!!

HARRY You ever hear of Anna Korenka?

QUINLAN The journalist? That's what this was all about?

VIVIAN Absolutely.

HARRY Well, that and the money.

VIVIAN The money mostly.

HARRY But her as well.

VIVIAN Her and the money!

VIVIAN HITS HIM HARD WITH THE GUN AND QUINLAN GOES DOWN, DISARMED.

HARRY Seriously, three citations for violence and you didn't see that coming?

VIVIAN GOES TO HARRY.

VIVIAN My god, you're bleeding?!

HARRY That's what happens when you get repeatedly hit in the face. Get me out of this thing.

SHE BEGINS TO UNTIE HIM, KEEPING AN EYE ON QUINLAN.

VIVIAN I think he killed Lazlo.

HARRY Uncle Felix? That's what you came up with? Uncle Felix?

VIVIAN It was a spur of the moment thing.

HARRY We're going to have to seriously work on your lying skills.

VIVIAN We'll have plenty of time to work on that.

HARRY 'We' we?

VIVIAN Us.

QUINLAN Mother fuck!

HARRY You got him.

VIVIAN I got him.

QUINLAN Mother fuck!

VIVIAN Sorry, Agent Quinlan, but only one person is allowed to torture Harry.

QUINLAN You hit me!

VIVIAN Move and I'll shoot you.

QUINLAN You motherfuckers! All this over a stupid journalist?

HARRY Anna? Anna wasn't a journalist.

QUINLAN What are you talking about? What was she then?

VIVIAN Anna Korenka never existed.

QUINLAN Who the fuck was shot on the steps of her apartment then?

VIVIAN That? That was our cleaning lady.

LIGHTS DOWN ON THEM, UP ON ANNA.

ANNA STANDS CENTRE STAGE. SHE LOOKS EXACTLY THE SAME AS BEFORE BUT NOW SPEAKS WITH A RUSSIAN ACCENT.

ENTER VIVIAN.

VIVIAN Ms. Karamav?

ANNA Ms. Marie?

VIVIAN Who?

ANNA   You are Ms. Marie?

VIVIAN Oh, right. Yes. English is okay?

ANNA   Da.

VIVIAN Not French?

ANNA   Niet.

VIVIAN No one speaks French anymore. So, you found the place okay?

ENTER HARRY.

HARRY Hi, sorry I'm late. Katya, yes?

ANNA   Da.

HARRY Did you find the place okay?

ANNA   How often you want me to clean?

HARRY Three times a week.

VIVIAN Except, there won't be any cleaning.

HARRY What my wife means is…

VIVIAN Your wife?

HARRY Well…

VIVIAN What my business associate means is that no one is going to be living here. We use the place for corporate receptions, things like that.

HARRY Some light dusting. Nothing more.

VIVIAN Oh, and if you could feed the cat.

HARRY (ASIDE) What cat.

VIVIAN There's a cat.

HARRY Why is there a cat?

VIVIAN Anna has a cat. She's a cat person.

HARRY Anna's an amalgam, what's an amalgam going to do with a cat?

VIVIAN I've always wanted a cat.

HARRY Then get one.

VIVIAN I'm allergic. It adds authenticity.

THE PAIR TURN BACK TO ANNA.

HARRY And feed the cat.

VIVIAN Felix.

HARRY And feed Felix.

ANNA You don't want me to clean?

VIVIAN No point.

HARRY Keep the heater on in winter. So the cat doesn't freeze. That sort of thing.

ANNA And for this you pay me?

HARRY Three thousand a month, okay?

VIVIAN It's very important you keep to these times though. You must be here three times a week and stay for the full time. You understand? You're free to relax but we are recording so any absence will be noticed.

ANNA Whatever.

HARRY (EXTENDING HIS HAND) Okay, Katya. It appears we have a deal.

ANNA Da.

EXIT ANNA.

HARRY Charming.

VIVIAN You sure this is necessary?

HARRY Business partner?

VIVIAN She seemed suspicious.

HARRY She's fine. If they put eyes on the place, there needs to be someone coming and going. You know, besides the cat.

VIVIAN (TURNING TO GO) That's that then. Leave the recorder in the bottom drawer of the bedroom. That's how we'll communicate. okay?

HARRY You're just going?

VIVIAN We can't be seen together.

HARRY But we have this lovely unchristened apartment!

VIVIAN This is too important.

HARRY Really?

VIVIAN What? What do you want to hear? It's not you, it's me? I respect our friendship too much to jeopardize it? You're like a brother to me? Does that do it for you? This is too important! Take the hint.

HARRY You don't mean that.

VIVIAN If we're going to do this, we can't be together. It's too much risk. You know that!

HARRY Then how come I feel like the most stupid man in the world right now.

LIGHTS UP, FULL STAGE LIT.

QUINLAN You pair are the most screwed up couple I've ever met, you know that.

VIVIAN (TURNING TO GO) Go home Agent Quinlan. You get a free pass. And no one gets to know that you were just about to sell your country out for the price of a small yacht. Go home.

VIVIAN TURNS HER BACK ON THEM. QUINLAN PULLS HIS KNIFE AND RUSHES HER.

QUINLAN Fuck you!

HARRY Vivian!

HARRY STEPS BETWEEN QUINLAN AND VIVIAN. UNSEEN BY VIVIAN HE'S STABBED BY QUINLAN WHO IS SHOT BY VIVIAN.

VIVIAN Harry!

HARRY SITS DOWN THE CHAIR. HE LOOKS HURT. VIVIAN RUSHES TO HIM.

VIVIAN (CONT.) What a piece of shit? Harry? Harry, you okay? Harry?

HARRY You know what the problem is with CIA safe houses? No guards.

VIVIAN Are you okay?

HARRY I'm fine. Winded.

VIVIAN We'd better get out of here. The FSB…

HARRY Hey. Hey. Before. What you said.

VIVIAN When?

HARRY About us. Now. After this.

VIVIAN I love you. I know it's stupid, I know it's pointless. But I love you, Harry. Is that what you want me to say?

HARRY It's what I want you to mean.

VIVIAN You really are the most stupid man I know, you know that. Come on. We've got to get out of here.

HARRY (PUSHING HER OFF) Not safe. We need to go separately. Once they find this place, Interpol will be looking for a couple. I'll meet you in rendezvous. Okay?

VIVIAN You sure?

HARRY I'm fine. I'll clear up the mess. Erase the tapes. Go! I'll see you there.

VIVIAN Five days.

EXIT VIVIAN.

HARRY Five days.

HARRY REACHES AROUND TO HIS BACK AND REMOVES QUINLAN'S KNIFE, COVERED IN BLOOD.

You cannot con an honest man. Actually, that's not true. You can con all the people all the time, some of the people some of the time, or the person you're living with whenever you want. You see, we all love a story. We're suckers for it. Something happens and within minutes we're turning it into an anecdote: for our friends, for our family, for Facebook, it's pretty much all the same thing. Doesn't matter if it's a car crash or a winning lottery ticket, we'll turn it into a story complete with synopsis and character profiles. We can't help it. We can't! Anything we can do to make a tidy little bow out of reality, we will. And if we can see that, if we can see the shape of a story in reality, then we'll believe it. No matter how far-fetched it actually is. Which is easier to believe: JFK was shot by a lone crazy man or the second shooter? We flew to the moon and found nothing there or the government set the whole thing up on a sound stage in Vermont? The bigger the lie, the easier the sell.

If you watch movies. If you watch the kind of movie where Bogart gets the dame and they do those spinning camera tricks that circle the table, you're led to believe that people like me can shuffle decks with their pinkies, move people like chess pieces, and read emotions off napkin papers... Alright, the last one's true but seriously; I've never even played blackjack. Con men are story tellers. We are tellers of tales and the tales we tell are the tales you want to hear. A long con, that's where you take a mark and you string him along until you get what you want, is nothing more than making the right story, the right situation. The mark is a character, an actor, living out the life he's always wanted to live. And trust me, right up until the great Oz, right up until the moment when the curtain is drawn back, there is no one happier than the mark.

We all do it in one way or another. A lie. A better version of reality. (BEAT) An affair. And sometimes we do it to ourselves. The greatest con we ever play? Love. And it's the ultimate in confidence tricks because the person we're taking into our confidence; is ourselves.

Love is the one great con we all play on the world and honestly, it can con anybody, anytime, anywhere.

SLUMPED IN THE CHAIR, HE DIES.

LIGHTS TO BLACKOUT.

SCENE 11

HARRY, ANNA AND VIVIAN ADDRESS THE AUDIENCE.

HARRY Letter to The Times – London, New York – copies to Economist, La Monde, Pravda. September 24th 2010.

ANNA Three months ago today I was shot in the head outside my apartment by someone who, I believe, was working in connection with the Russian mafia, under the guidance of the CIA.

VIVIAN Details of my death, including proof of those responsible are available to anyone upon request. All I require in return... All I ask from my sacrifice... is that the whole truth is printed – without omissions – so that the guilty can be brought to justice and my death and the deaths of so many others like me, will not have been in vain.

EXIT HARRY AND ANNA.

VIVIAN IS LEFT STANDING ALONE ON THE STAGE.

UNSEEN BY HER, LAZLO, DRESSED AS A RABBI, ENTERS AND STANDS NEXT TO HER.

ANNOUNCER Flight call, nine one seven for Istanbul now boarding. All passengers please make your way to the gate for departure.

LAZLO So, I think to myself. I think. Who benefits? This is what I think. I think. Who is going to get something out of this? What are they trying to get out of this? Revenge? I did not kill your friend the reporter. Mr. Hand pulls the trigger. I am the brain, yes, but even the brain is slave to the heart. This is the way of things, yes? Revenge against me is pointless. And then I think; brain is slave to the heart! It's love!!! You love him, he loves you. He is conman, you are spy.

This is never going to work. So you concoct great scenario so you have to work together! Sure, he comes up with it, but you want him to come up with it! You want him to stop you from doing the right thing. Am I right? I am right. Love, yes love, I think and this I am alright with. Love is good reason for doing things. It is pure. So, I got shot. For love? This is not so much. True love is worth everything. (PAUSE, THEN A SIGH) And then I check my bank accounts.

VIVIAN I thought Quinlan killed you.

LAZLO Meh, when you are trying to leave the Russian mafia is good idea to wear kevlar. Still…

VIVIAN Why are you dressed like a rabbi?

LAZLO Not dressed as. I am rabbi! Ist good, yeah? To the world, I am dead. To the mafia, I am dead. My grandmother, she already live in Jerusalem. I have papers, they make me a citizen. It's good. I do some intelligence work for Mossad in the nights but in the day, Rabbi. I am like Batman, only fetushed. Where is my money?

VIVIAN Where's Harry?

LAZLO Dead. (PAUSE) Okay, I should have put that a little kinder, I'm sorry. Good man. Died in the safe house. But then, you know this, yes? You knew it the moment you left the safe house.

VIVIAN The FSB…

LAZLO Yes, I know. You had to make it out of Russia. But still you come here, still you hope. He was not the only one to love I see. Where is my money?

VIVIAN Where you'll never find it.

LAZLO I found you. (PAUSE) He really loved you, you know? To want to die alone like that? Very special type of man. I was married twenty years and I faked my own death to get the hell away from her. Still, maybe that's the point.

VIVIAN He was a confidence trickster.

LAZLO And he put his confidence in you. (SIGH) Jerusalem is very beautiful this time of year, don't you think?

VIVIAN I'm not going to Jerusalem.

LAZLO No? It's a pity. Jerusalem is safe for you. Good work, purpose. Mossad say they are very interested in a woman with your... sensibilities.

VIVIAN Why would I work with anyone who works with you?

LAZLO Interpol, they after you. CIA, they after you. You are not Harry. Yes? Harry, he could have avoided them, but you... You are not Harry. Even with all my money.

VIVIAN You're not having it back.

LAZLO Meh. It's only money. Rabbi does lots of bar mitzvah, is not problem.

ANNOUNCER Gates now closing for flight nine one seven for Istanbul. Gates closing for flight nine one seven for Istanbul.

VIVIAN I get a new identity?

LAZLO License to kill.

VIVIAN Dental?

LAZLO Goes without saying.

VIVIAN (PAUSE) You have a plane?

THE PAIR TURN TO LEAVE.

LAZLO This...

VIVIAN Don't say it.

LAZLO What? You don't know what I'm going to say!

VIVIAN We studied your every move for three months. We stole a billion dollars off you. You think I don't know what you're going to say next?

LAZLO I was just going to say...

VIVIAN Don't say it.

EXIT LAZLO AND VIVIAN.

LAZLO ....that this could be the beginning of a beautiful friendship.

THERE IS A GUNSHOT OFF STAGE.

VIVIAN (OFF) I told you not to say it.

END OF ACT 2.

CURTAINS.

THE END.

CUT SCENES

Performed in Cambridge in 2010 the original production
of the play contained two extra scenes (not in order).
Although enjoyable,they were regarded as superfluous to
the overall structure of the play.
They are presented here for the first time outside the
Cambridge performance.

SCENE 5

RAIN STARTS AGAIN.

LIGHTS UP.

ENTER ANNA.

SHE IS HOLDING A 'MISSING CAT' POSTER.

SHE SIGHS AND PULLS OUT THE VOICE RECORDER. CLICKING IT ON SHE HEARS HER OWN VOICE.

ANNA (RECORDED) '…More frightening still however, is the West's ambivalent attitude to such alliances, with either a blind eye or a blank check given to anyone with even the most…'

ANNA (CONT.) Learn to write. (SHE CLICKS THE RECORDER ON AND STARTS TALKING) Anna tapes, 275. (BEAT) The growing influence of Russia on global stability is increasingly dismissed in the west. New Paragraph. While the Cold War was seen as the peak of Russian influence, the truth remains that communism was, at least, easy to spot. Now, however, Russia and Putin's government are just one more in a series of international capital markets and the insidiousness… okay, that might not be a real word, check that… the insidiousness of their behavior is often missed in a global marketplace already full of insidious behavior. Full stop, new Paragraph. This is not simply to be seen in the incessant vetoes in the UN where, bridged with China, Russia manages to stop anything that could threaten its economic expansion. Zimbabwe alone… You know, skip down, I'll come back to that. Note to self. Check with Vanity Fair how many words they're allowing for the piece. (BEAT) New paragraph. The recent deal with Cuba over oil drilling will net Russia over twenty two billion barrels of oil in an already depressed market and… You know what, I can't concentrate in this mess. So, if you're listening to this, (SHOUTS) tidy up for once in your life you little boy!

SCENE 8

LIGHTS UP ON LAZLO AND HARRY SITTING AND TALKING AT A TABLE. HAND IS AT ANOTHER TABLE READING AN OVERTLY LITERARY BOOK. THERE ARE PHOTOS ON THE

TABLE.

HARRY Echelon is, at its most basic, information sharing between countries. Data mining. But in reality it's big brother personified. Satellite surveillance. Electronic eavesdropping. Your phone, your mobile phone. Anything you can use to send sound or video can be used to eavesdrop on your conversation. Even now, switched off, your mobile is still capable of transmitting micro waves and, with the right equipment, being used to listen in to everything you say, and everything you do.

LAZLO PICKS THE PHONE UP, DROPS IT ON THE FLOOR, AND SMASHES IT WITH HIS FOOT.

HARRY (CONT.) Yes, well. You could have just taken the battery out. But, hey, that way was effective as well. But it doesn't stop there. A team in London just discovered a way to piggyback a signal onto your home electrical current which means that basically, any sound you make, any conversation you have at home, near an electrical outlet, is able to be intercepted. This isn't science fiction, this is science fact. (PICKING UP THE PHOTOS) These photos? Keyhole satellite.

LAZLO (PICKING UP A PHOTO) Even on toilet?

HARRY Even on the toilet. Every time you walk out the door, you're on camera. Every conversation you have in a public place, in the privacy of your own home, they can intercept. Privacy is the product of a past generation. America denies Echelon's existence but Europe's already testified that it exists. The only thing you can hope is that what you're doing, whatever illegal things you've got going on, aren't more important to them than you knowing they know… if you know what I mean.

LAZLO Then why send me the photos?

HARRY That is the question. Obviously someone wants you to know they know. They want you to know they have access to you whenever they want. Do you have any major deals coming up?

LAZLO Apart from buying Arsenal?

HARRY No. For something that size it would have to be… Something you're doing would have to be of threat to them, and by them, I mean, the United States. No way the U.S. would let any of the Euros play a hand this big. Is anything you're doing a threat to American business interests?

LAZLO Nothing.

HARRY Anything you've done recently?

LAZLO (PAUSE) How do you stop it?

HARRY You can't.

LAZLO I...

HARRY You can't! There's no way to get off the grid. No way. Go live in cabin in the middle of the Australian outback, but if you want to live amongst the real people; nothing. Only thing you can do is make them want to stop watching you.

LAZLO How?

HARRY Why does anyone do anything? Self interest! You're married. What do you do when you want your wife to, I don't know, have sex with you? I don't mean quick, married sex, I mean weekend-long, no holds barred, bring the roof down sex. You know, single sex.

LAZLO I buy her a yacht. She has a lot of yacht.

HARRY Alright. But let's say you don't have, you know, several billion dollars. What do you do then? You trick her. You make her want to have sex with you. And how do you do that? It depends, right? Maybe you make her jealous, nothing works like jealousy. Maybe you make her feel guilty. Or maybe, maybe you trick her into thinking that not having sex with you is a really bad thing.

LAZLO Yacht is much easier.

HARRY Alright, forget the analogy. Think of it like this. Reality is perception. We're not frightened by what we can see. We can see it, we can shoot it, spoil it, turn it to our own advantages. We're frightened by what we haven't thought of. The best looking woman is the one you haven't had yet. The best technology is the one that doesn't yet exist. No way to fight what doesn't exist. If the United States believe that you have something, something that is detrimental to their spy technology, then they won't dare use that spy technology against you. If they think you have something, a metal perhaps, that can disrupt... everything, then, in effect, you'd become a no-fly zone.

LAZLO And you can do this?

HARRY Reality is perception. The more important question is what do they already know, and for that, you'd need to get inside Echelon itself and that... is where the clever part comes in.

ORIGINAL
ARTWORK

LOVE IS NOT NEARLY AS SATISFYING AS

MURDER ME GENTLY

RETRIBUTION

THE GAMES BEGIN MARCH 2011

ORIGINAL FLYER (FRONT)

FROM THE PEOPLE WHO BROUGHT YOU THE INTERNATIONALLY ACCLAIMED 'CROSSROADS COUNTRY', COMES THE SHOW OF THE SUMMER.

When a Russian journalist is shot dead on her doorstep, a Conman and an Interpol agent unite to wreak revenge on the people they believe responsible; the Russian Mafia and the C.I.A.

But while all's fair in love and war, little is even civil in the world of international espionage.

Who's fooling who? Who's on whose side? And what wouldn't you give to torture an ex?

In the classic tradition of Film Noir comes a romantic thriller/comedy that pits nation against nation, friend against foe and sex against sex in a global game of cat and mouse that could affect us all.

Set around the startling true stories of the murder and assassination of Russian Journalists such as Alexander Litvinenko and Anna Politkovskaya as well as the up-to-the-minute headline of Russian sleeper spies caught in the U.S and the invasion of Georgia, the play blends reality and fiction to help illuminate the abuses of human rights and military oppression systemic in modern day Russia.

WWW.MURDERMEGENTLY.COM

MUMFORD THEATRE - CAMBRIDGE

7.30pm Thurs Sept 23th, Fri 24th, Sat 25th 2010	Adult £12
2.30pm Sat Sept 25th	Concessions £ 8

About Mumford

The Mumford Theatre is situated within the heart of the Anglia Ruskin University campus. To find the theatre, walk down to the end of Broad Street, adjacent to Anglia Ruskin, and turn right into the campus. Walk straight ahead and enter the rear of the Mumford Building on the right through the shared Theatre/Library entrance.

MURDER

  **ME**

 **GENTLY**

WWW.MURDERMEGENTLY.COM

ADDITIONAL FLYER FOR LONDON PREMIER

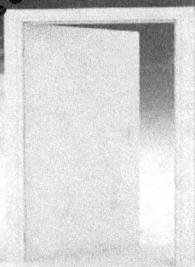

MURDER ME GENTLY

Also by

DIRECT

LIGHT

THOMAS ALEXANDER

THOMAS ALEXANDER

THE VISITOR

By

THOMAS ALEXANDER

THE VISITOR

WHEN THE LOVER OF A FAMOUS WRITER GOES MISSING IN A WAR RAVAGED COUNTRY HE BRIBES HIS WAY INTO A JAIL TO QUESTION HER HUSBAND, A MISSIONARY, WHO IS BEING TORTURED AS A TRAINING EXERCISE BY HIS CAPTORS.

ALONE IN THE CELL, THE TWO START A DIALOGUE ABOUT THE NATURE OF BELIEF.

BELIEF IN GOD, LOVE, AND POLITICS.

MURDER ME GENTLY

BY

THOMAS ALEXANDER

"ONE MAN... ONE WOMAN... AND THE QUEST FOR JUSTICE IN AN UNJUST WORLD"

MODERN DAY RUSSIA THROUGH THE MEDIUM OF FILM NOIR

BLENDING REAL LIFE EVENTS WITH COMEDY AND INTRIGUE, *MURDER ME GENTLY*'S UNIQUE PERSPECTIVE ON THE WORLD OF RUSSIAN POLITICS AS SEEN THROUGH THE LENS OF FLIM NOIR, SPANS THE ASSASINATION OF INTERNATIONALLY RENOWNED JOURNALISTS, PUTIN'S REACH FOR THE RETURN OF SOVIET SATELLITE STATES, AND THE INFLITRATION OF GOVERNMENT BY OLIGARCHS AND CRIMINALS.

PROVIDING A DAMMING INDICTMENT OF THE WEST'S INABILITY TO HALT MOSCOW'S POLICY OF EXPANSIONISM *MURDER ME GENTLY* LENDS A THEATRICAL EXPOSE TO THE VERY REAL WORLD OF CORRUPTION AND GREED IN INTERNATIONAL POLITICS TODAY.

A CONMAN, A DISGRACED INTERPOL AGENT, A MAFIA BOSS, A CIA SPOOK, AND THE SECRET TO THE FUTURE ALL UNITE IN AN UNLIKELY ALLIANCE IN A LOVE AFFAIR THAT WILL DEFINE THE FATE OF THE WORLD IN THOMAS ALEXANDER'S

... MURDER ME ... GENTLY!

97

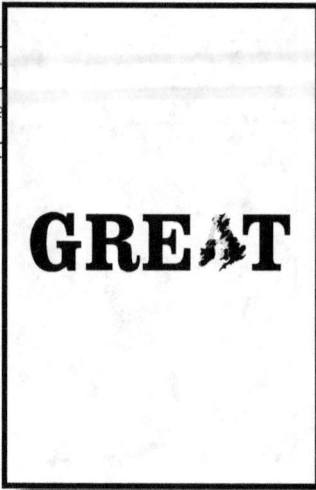

GREAT

GREAT

BY

THOMAS ALEXANDER

A REMOTE ROOM IN THE THROES OF WINTER.

THE ONCE GREAT MAN LIVES ALONE NOW WITH HIS SON,

AN OLD FRIEND HAS COME TO VISIT. HE HAS CLIMBED UP FROM THE VILLAGE IN ORDER TO OFFER THE OLD MAN ONE LAST CHANCE TO ESCAPE THE ENCROACHING WINTER THAT IS ABOUT TO TAKE HIM, STIRRING UP MEMORIES OF BETTER TIMES AND THE WARMTH OF SUMMER.

BEGAT

BY

THOMAS ALEXANDER

By Thomas Alexander

IN A COUNTRY, AFTER THE WAR, A JUDGE THROWS A DINNER PARTY, SEEKING SUPPORT AGAINST A POWERFUL MINISTER WHO HAS RAPED AND KILLED A SERVANT GIRL.

BUT THE JUDGE HIMSELF IS THE TARGET TONIGHT, AND THE SHADOW OF THE WAR HE SO DESPERATELY WANTS TO LEAVE BEHIND THREATENS TO ENGULF HIS FAMILY AS A YOUNG WOMAN SEEKS REVENGE FOR THE SINS OF HIS PAST.

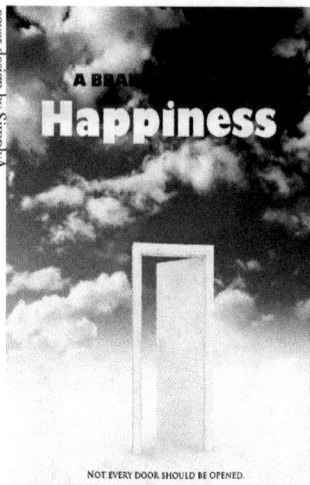

HAPPINESS

BY

THOMAS ALEXANDER

ON A REMOTE HEADLAND IN NORTH WALES A MAN AND HIS PARAPLEGIC SON DREAM OF LIFE BEYOND THE CONFINES OF THEIR FOUR WALLS.

BUT WHEN A WOMAN OFFERS THEM THE ESCAPE THEY SO CRAVE THEY FIND THEY ARE BOUND BY MORE THEN THEIR DREAMS.

THE JEALOUSY OF A BORED POLICE-MAN AND THE KINDNESS OF A MAIL ORDER BRIDE SET THEM ON A PATH OF HOPE AND DESTRUCTION.

THE LAST CHRISTMAS

THE LAST CHRISTMAS

BY

THOMAS ALEXANDER

IT'S NEWS!

WHEN AN EMBATTLED NEWSROOM RECEIVES A POTENTIALLY EARTH SHATTERING STORY MINUTES BEFORE AIR ON CHRISTMAS DAY THE CAREFUL EQUILIBRIUM OF THE TEAM IS SHATTERED AND OLD DIVIDING LINES COME TO THE FORE, TURNING CO-WORKER AGAINST CO-WORKER.

SET IN REAL TIME AND INCORPORATING ACTUAL AND INTERCHANGEABLE NEWS EVENTS THE LAST CHRISTMAS PITS SOCIAL POLITICS AGAINST JOURNALISTIC INTEGRITY IN A BATTLE OF THE ETHICS.

GOD

By

Thomas Alexander

When the named partner of a small law firm dies, leaving large debt, the remaining misfits of the firm are forced to take on just about any client available, including a litigious soccer-mum who would like to sue God for the death of her husband – hit by a lightning bolt on the 15th hole of a municipal golf course.

The Trial becomes complicated however, when an indigent with no background and a canny knack of knowing everyone's background enters the courtroom claiming to be God.

Batting back and fore between the courtroom and the personal lives of the lawyers, God is a fast paced courtroom drama/comedy that uses original staging and non-linear storytelling to provide a lighthearted, but complex social drama.

THE FAMILY

BY

THOMAS ALEXANDER

TODAY, FOR THE FIRST TIME IN LONGER THAN ANYONE CAN REMEMBER, THE FAMILY ARE GATHERING. THEY ARE GATHERING TO CELEBRATE THE ENGAGEMENT OF THE MATERNAL NIECE, THEY ARE GATHERING TO CELEBRATE THE LAST BIRTHDAY OF THE PATRIARCH, THEY ARE GATHERING TO WELCOME HOME THE PRODIGAL SON AND HIS BEAUTIFUL GIRLFRIEND, AND THEY ARE GOING TO CELEBRATE ALL THIS WITH A SLIDE-SHOW.

CANDID PHOTOGRAPHS. PHOTOGRAPHS OF THINGS NO ONE THOUGHT ANYONE ELSE KNEW ABOUT. PHOTOGRAPH TAKEN WHEN NO ONE ELSE WAS THERE.

IT'S ALL COMING OUT TODAY. IN BLACK AND WHITE FOR EVERYONE TO SEE. THE REMNANTS OF CHILD ABUSE, INFIDELITY, LOSS, DESTRUCTION, AND MISSED BIRTHDAY PARTIES. IT'S ALL COMING OUT. IT'S GOING TO BE A LONG NIGHT. POSSIBLY FOREVER.

THE RECRUITMENT OFFICER

By

THOMAS ALEXANDER

TOM, A CHARMING YANKEE RECRUITER, COMES TO AN UNSPECIFIED ENGLISH TOWN AND FALLS IN LOVE WITH THE CONFERENCE CENTRE MANAGER, JULIA.

BUT WHAT EXACTLY IS HE RECRUITING FOR? WHY DOES EVERYONE WHO JOINS NEVER COME BACK AND WHAT IS ON THE OTHER SIDE OF THE DOOR

WHERE DO THE RECRUITS GO AFTER SIGNING UP?

AN EXISTENTIAL LOVE STORY THAT ASKS QUESTIONS OF WHO WE ARE, WHAT WE WANT FROM LIFE, AND WHETHER WE'RE GETTING IT, THE RECRUITMENT OFFICER IS A REMODELLING OF THE 1706 PLAY BY GEORGE FARQUHAR. *THE RECRUITING OFFICER.*

WRITER'S BLOCK

BY

THOMAS ALEXANDER

PAUL BLOCK WAS ONCE A PROLIFIC WRITER. A RECIPIENT OF BOTH THE PEN AND FAULKNER-AWARDS AND THE AUTHOR OF OVER TEN DIFFERENT NOVELS, HE WAS ONCE CONSIDERED THE UK'S MOST UP AND COMING WRITER UNTIL, AT THE AGE OF FORTY, HE SUFFERED A NERVOUS BREAKDOWN.

TEN YEARS LATER THE WORLD HAS FORGOTTEN PAUL BLOCK. HOLED UP IN HIS STUDY HE HAS BEEN WORKING ON THE SAME FIRST PAGE OF HIS NEW NOVEL FOR NEARLY FIVE YEARS, KEPT COMPANY BY ONLY HIS MAID, A FOUL MOUTHED IRISH HIT-MAN, A VETERAN OF THE BATTLE OF GETTYSBURG AND A NINETEEN FORTIES FEMME FATALE.

TODAY, ALL THAT'S GOING TO CHANGE. PAUL HAS A BUSY DAY AHEAD OF HIM. FIRST HE'S GOING TO KILL A PERSISTENT AND CHARMLESS YOUNG REPORTER WHO WANTS TO DO A PIECE ON 'WRITER'S BLOCK' AND THEN HE'S GOING TO HAVE A RARE VISIT FROM HIS SON WHO'S BRINGING HIM BAD NEWS AND A NEW COUCH.

WITH A MISSING BODY AND A SON WHO HATES HIM, PAUL MUST FINALLY RID HIMSELF OF HIS PROTAGONISTS IF HE'S EVER GOING TO STAY OUT OF JAIL, AND FINISH THAT FIRST PAGE.

THOMAS

Japan, 1945 – A Family At War

When a wandering priest escaping a troubled past is taken in by a prominent family, a quiet city in northern Japan is forced to confront the dark shadows of war seeping into their lives in ways they could never have anticipated.

With its townsmen scattered throughout the farthest ends of a desperate empire in a final defence against the encroaching West, the idyllic northern city of Morioka, far removed from the harsh realities of the front, is largely left to itself.

THOMAS ALEXANDER

A Scattering of Orphans

But when a prominent doctor is conscripted and sent to Manila, his sister is left as head of the household and must deal with a young priest living at the bottom of their garden with a large collection of maps and strange knowledge of English.

As the cold hand of war approaches, each person must choose their own destiny and place in the new world.

THE OTHER SIDE

ALEXANDER

Commemorating the 70th Anniversary of the end of WW2! A trilogy spanning the length of the war from the viewpoint of an ordinary Japanese family.

Thomas Alexander

The Disingenuous Martyr

omas Alexander

Beyond The Noonday Sun

Offering a unique perspective through the eyes of a rural Japanese family into the impact of history's bloodiest war to date, *A Scattering of Orphans* is one family's attempt to make sense of a changing world amidst the desolation of war, both home and abroad.

DIRECT
LIGHT

OF THE SUN

DIRECT LIGHT

THOMAS ALEXANDER